Time for a Better Marriage

Time for a Better Marriage

Don Dinkmeyer & Jon Carlson

AGS ®
American Guidance Service,
Circle Pines, Minnesota 55014-1796

*AGS staff participating in the development
and production of this publication:*

Program Development
Dorothy Chapman, *Director*
Diane LeTendre, *Art Director*

Product Development
David Youngquist, *Director*
Rosanne Hagen, *Production Coordinator*
Diane Kuhrmeyer, *Production Coordinator*
Maureen Wilson, *Art Director*

Project Editor
Gerri Johnson

Illustrations
John Bush

Cover and book design
Terry Dugan, *Terry Dugan Design*

Printed in the United States of America.

Library of Congress Catalog Card Number: 83-073510

ISBN 0-913476-64-1

A 0 9 8 7 6

Thanks to E. Jane and Laura
for giving us time.

This time like all times is a very good one
if we but know what to do with it.

Ralph Waldo Emerson

CONTENTS

Introduction

Time for a Better Marriage is a program designed to help you better understand your marriage and learn important skills that will enable you to enrich your relationship. Basic to the development of this program are the following principles:

1. *Developing and maintaining a good marital relationship requires a time commitment.* For your marriage relationship to succeed, you must make it an important priority now and in the future.

2. *Specific skills that are essential to a healthy marriage can be learned.* When you understand how a marriage works and the necessary skills for building a successful marriage, you can develop the skills that create a positive, rewarding relationship.

3. *Change often takes time, but all change begins with you.* The first step in enriching a marriage involves a commitment to change. You begin by understanding what your role in the marriage has been and what you can do to make it different. Be patient in your growth and allow for different rates of change. As you proceed through the program, some weeks will produce wonders and others will produce little apparent change.

4. *Feelings of love and caring that have diminished or disappeared often return when behavior changes.* Romantic feelings, intimacy, and love often diminish over time in a marriage relationship. When feelings change, many couples believe that the relationship is over. This need not be the case. A change of feelings may mean that you and your partner are not being reinforced in the marriage and that the relationship deserves a higher priority. It is important at such times to act *as if* all were well. By acting *as if* your relationship is the intimate, satisfying relationship you desire, new behaviors and feelings can be established.

5. *Small changes are very important in bringing about big changes.* A happier relationship results from many small changes over a period of time. Even though both you and your partner are committed to change, there may be times when unwanted patterns reappear. This does not mean that the new skills you are learning are not working in your marriage. Continue to focus on the positive relationship you desire and these times of testing will pass.

The Best Use of *Time for a Better Marriage*

Each chapter in *Time for a Better Marriage* helps you learn an important skill. We recommend that you read the chapters and work through the exercises in the order presented to gain the fullest advantage from the sequential presentation of skills. Begin your study by making a commitment, individually and as a couple, to spend the time and effort required to put into action the skills presented.

Set aside regular times for reading and doing the exercises. Plan your sessions in advance. Plan to cover one chapter per week. Most couples find that they will need two hours each week to work on the assignments. Get out your calendars and begin to set aside time for individual reading and sessions together. Consider joining or forming a group to study with other couples.*

Part of your time commitment should be reserved for three important activities: Daily Dialogue (introduced in Chapter 1), Encouragement Meetings (introduced in Chapter 2), and Marriage Meetings (introduced in Chapter 6).

Throughout the book you will find suggestions for exercises to do as a couple. We suggest the following guidelines for your discussions:

1. Give your full attention to what your partner is saying. This is not the time to plan your response to what your partner is saying.

Time for a Better Marriage is available as a program for group study. A form in the back of your book will assist you in locating groups.

2. Your goal is to understand, not necessarily to agree. You are each entitled to your own feelings, attitudes, and beliefs. Some differences can be resolved and others must be dismissed with the understanding that it is perfectly okay to agree to disagree.

3. Accept what your partner says without feeling you must take a position. Listen with the goal of understanding. Do not criticize, attack, or defend yourself.

4. Before responding to your partner, ask yourself, "Do I really understand? If I don't understand, what do I need help with?"

Reinforcing Your Skills

In the back of this book you will find two sheets with tear-out cards that will guide your progress in this program. The *Daily Focus Cards* suggest activities that will help you apply your new understanding and skills on a daily basis. The cards reinforce what you are learning and help you practice new behaviors so that they become familiar and are more likely to become a part of your life. The *Marriage Skill Cards* help you quickly locate information specific to one of the important new skills you've learned. For example, there are cards summarizing the procedure for Daily Dialogue, Marriage Meetings, and Encouragement Meetings. The skill cards are a tool to help reinforce the skills you are learning in your reading, activities, and sharing time. Tear them out and wear them out!

Keeping Track of Your Progress

Many important things are going to happen during your experience in using *Time for a Better Marriage*. When we are in the middle of a new learning experience it is hard to believe we will forget the valuable understanding and skills that we are learning. But we can lose some of the information if we do not have a way of storing it. To reinforce your new skills, take a few minutes each week to write down your new understanding and perceptions and what you plan to do as a result of what you have learned. To help you keep track of your progress we have included a form at the end of each chapter, MY PLAN. MY PLAN helps you focus each week on the specific skills you are learning in *Time for a Better Marriage* and encourages you to plan ways to put your new understanding into action during the following week.

You may also wish to keep a log, or journal, in which you write about what you are learning and decisions that you are making. Review your journal on a weekly basis. By keeping track of the positive changes that result from your reading you will reap benefits long after your study is completed.

It is our hope that *Time for a Better Marriage* provides you with the encouragement and skills you need to build the marriage relationship you really desire.

Don Dinkmeyer, Ph.D.

Jon Carlson, Ed.D.

Diplomate of Counseling Psychology,
   American Board of Professional Psychology
Diplomate, Marital and Family Therapy,
   American Board of Family Psychology
Clinical Member, American Association for
   Marriage and Family Therapy
President, Communication and Motivation
   Training Institute, Inc. (CMTI),
   Coral Springs, Florida

Diplomate, Marital and Family Therapy,
   American Board of Family Psychology
Clinical Member, American Association for
   Marriage and Family Therapy
Assistant Clinical Professor,
   Department of Preventative Medicine,
   Medical College of Wisconsin
Psychologist, Lake Geneva Wellness Clinic,
   Lake Geneva, Wisconsin

How do you feel about your marriage today?

A Good Marriage Begins With You

When you said "to have and to hold, until death do us part" you expressed what you hoped your marriage would bring—a sense of belonging. But how can you nurture that sense of belonging to ensure that in one year—or ten, or twenty, or fifty years—your marriage will be exciting and satisfying? Lasting, exciting, and satisfying marriages are created when marriage partners love and support each other. The question becomes, how can you love and support each other more often? Like muscles, love and support become stronger with exercise.

There are many factors that can interfere with a relationship and many skills that can help create an atmosphere of love and support. The skills necessary for creating and sustaining an effective marriage are learned. This is a guide to help you understand your marriage relationship and to learn those important skills that make it work.

You began marriage with an assortment of skills, some effective and others ineffective in helping you achieve the desired sense of belonging. The skills needed to enrich your marriage can be expressed in simple terms. In an exciting, satisfying marriage partners relate in these positive ways:

- They individually accept responsibility for their behavior and their self-esteem.
- They identify and align their personal and marital goals.
- They choose to encourage each other.
- They communicate their feelings with honesty and openness.
- They listen empathetically when feelings are being expressed.

- They seek to understand the factors that influence their relationship.
- They demonstrate that they accept and value each other.
- They choose thoughts, words, and actions that support the positive goals of their marriage.
- They solve marital conflicts.
- They commit themselves to the ongoing process of maintaining an equal marriage.

How Can I Begin to Enrich My Marriage?

Each partner plays an important role in creating an atmosphere of love and support, or in sustaining marital conflict. If either partner changes to a more effective pattern of behavior, the other partner has to respond differently. A good marriage begins with you! The first step in enriching your marriage relationship is to accept responsibility for your behavior. When you accept responsibility for your behavior, you are acknowledging that you have power—the power to choose.

Power to Choose

We all have the power to choose our beliefs, feelings, and attitudes. As we acknowledge this power, we begin to move to a more meaningful level of relating. Many individuals deny this power by saying, "I can't." It would be more accurate to say, "I do not choose to." "I can't" is a helpless response; "I choose" or "I choose not to" implies strength and self-control.

Although we cannot control all of the circumstances in our marriage, we can control the attitude we take toward our marriage. Like the poker player, we can't choose our cards, but we can choose how to play the hand. Choose to believe that you can build a more satisfying, exciting relationship.

Are you choosing to make your marriage successful?

BUT, ARETHA, YOU TOLD ME TO GET SOME EXERCISE!

When we accept responsibility for our own behavior, we free ourselves of the need to blame or make excuses.

Develop a Blame-free Lifestyle

When we accept responsibility for our behavior, our feelings, and our problems, we can channel our energy and time toward the positive goals of marriage rather than using energy to make excuses and find someone to blame.

What excuses have you used that keep you from changing your behavior?

Have you blamed your partner for problems in your marriage?

Have you blamed yourself?

Are there other circumstances in your marriage that you have felt are to blame for the shortcomings in your relationship?

Develop the Courage to be Imperfect

If we continually strive for perfection, life can seem very unfulfilling. We may find ourselves in a continual state of feeling inadequate or inferior. Feelings of inferiority and inadequacy are major sources of discouragement that we all experience at some time. However, if we recognize that we are human, and therefore make mistakes, we can eliminate a major source of discouragement in our lives and in our marriage. Freed from the need to be perfect, we can begin to take risks. We can begin to participate and contribute without the pressure of perfectionism defeating us before we begin.

As you develop the courage to be imperfect, you will be more realistic about yourself and your partner. Rather than feeling discouraged, you can begin to identify ways to change.

In what areas of your marriage have you been expecting perfection of yourself or your partner?

Will Power

When someone is confronted with either the need to eliminate a bad habit or begin a good habit, we often hear the expression, "I just don't have the will power." Most of us recognize areas in our marriage where we would like to change our behavior, but we often excuse ourselves with the statement, "I'd like to change, but I can't seem to do it."

When we do not make desired changes, we are resisting. Resistance may take many forms: active or passive, total or partial, overt or covert. Resistance is usually a reflexive action, but it can be controlled. To overcome resistance to change, we decide how we really want to react to a given situation. Think about ways you can use your strong will and determination to bring about positive changes in your marriage. The question is not "Can I?" but "Do I want to?" The following dialogue between a counselor and client illustrates the role of will power.

Counselor: Do you think you could find time to spend with your wife if I paid you five dollars a day?

Client: I doubt it.

Counselor: How about one hundred dollars a day?

Client: [After long pause] I don't know.

Counselor: Could you do it if I paid you five hundred dollars a day?

Client: [Instant response] I sure could!

Counselor: Well, do it then.

Client: [Smiling] Will you pay me the five hundred dollars a day?

Counselor: Of course not.

Client: I'd like to, but I can't.

Counselor: We have already established that you can—it's just a matter of price.

If you are motivated enough, you can change. You have the will power. You need to develop the *want* power.

Self-discipline

Self-discipline can help you overcome your resistance to change in all areas of your life. Two areas that require self-discipline are exercise and relaxation. Partners who take time for exercise and take time alone for relaxation feel good, look good, and manage stress more effectively. The rewards of self-discipline are quickly apparent.

Regular exercise programs should include activities that increase cardiovascular fitness, strength, and flexibility. Plan to exercise at least three times a week. Two good sources of information that can help you set up a personal exercise program are Ken Cooper's *The Aerobics Program for Total Well-Being*,[1] and Gay Hendricks and Jon Carlson's *The Centered Athlete*.[2]

Allot time alone for yourself and encourage and preserve your partner's opportunity for time alone as well. Time alone allows you the opportunity to relax and to manage stress. Choose a relaxation procedure such as napping, transcendental meditation, self-hypnosis, prayer, or reading. The authors have prepared a cassette containing relaxation exercises.* Also, helpful information on relaxation techniques can be found in Lawrence LeShan's *How to Meditate*[3] and Jon Carlson's *The Basics of Stress Management*.[4]

As you accept responsibility for your behavior, recognize that you have the power to choose, and develop the courage to be imperfect, you demonstrate self-love and self-understanding. And self-discipline reinforces good feelings about yourself. As you love and understand yourself more, you are better able to accept your partner's love and to give love in return.

Allot time alone for yourself and encourage and preserve your partner's time alone as well.

Understanding Marital Behavior

Behavior is neither random nor meaningless. All behavior is directed, knowingly or unknowingly, toward the achievement of a goal. The word

---

*The cassette, *Time to Relax and Imagine*, is available from American Guidance Service, Circle Pines, MN. An order form is provided in the back of this book.

goal in this context means an individual's psychological motivation. In any given situation, we *choose* how to respond. The response we choose depends on our goal. Our goal may be conscious or unconscious. If we know what our goal is, we can choose behaviors that support the goal. However, if we have a goal that we are not aware of, our behaviors may be helping us reach a goal that is not in our best interests or in the best interests of our marriage relationship. For example, if we always have to have the last word in an argument, our need for this type of power may keep an argument going even though, for our marriage relationship, the most beneficial action at the time would be to withdraw from the argument. Therefore, to understand marital behavior, we must first identify what we hope to achieve by our behavior. In other words, what is our goal?

In general, in a satisfying marriage a couple chooses behaviors that help them achieve positive goals for their relationship. Their choices create and sustain the desired sense of belonging. In other words, their behaviors are effective.

Why are some couples more able to choose effective behaviors than others? The behaviors necessary for creating and sustaining an effective mar-

riage are learned. There are, however, few models of healthy marriage relationships. Too often the models available to us teach us what we do *not* want from our marriage relationship. Television, books, and magazines are filled with examples of unhappy couples in extramarital escapades. We are fortunate if we have friends and relatives whose marriages serve as good models. Given the relative absence of models of truly satisfying marriages, it is not surprising that many couples have not learned to choose effective behaviors that are vital in enriching a marriage.

Goals of Positive Marital Behavior

In an enriched marriage relationship a couple chooses to act in ways that nourish the sense of belonging each partner desires. Rather than acting solely out of self-interest, the couple chooses behaviors that support positive goals of marriage. There are four positive goals that foster good marriage relationships. They are:

1. To accept responsibility for individual behavior
2. To cooperate
3. To contribute to the relationship
4. To encourage each other

Chart 1A

Goals of Positive Marital Behavior

Goal	Feelings/Beliefs	Behavior
To be responsible.	I am responsible for my own behavior. Our marriage can be satisfying.	Accepts responsibility for marital problems. Volunteers to help partner.
To contribute.	I can belong by contributing. I feel adequate and loved by partner.	Communicates honestly. Does own work. Initiates social and sexual activity. Shows self-discipline.
To cooperate.	I am more interested in cooperating with my partner than getting even or winning.	Returns kindness for hurt. Ignores hurts. Asks self, "What can I do to improve the situation?" Accepts imperfections.
To encourage.	I feel liked and treated fairly. I do not need to fight and tear my partner down. I choose to build my partner up.	Sees partner's assets more often than weaknesses. Encourages partner. Listens to partner.

How does a goal influence a couple's pattern of relating? **Chart 1A** illustrates the relationship of a goal to an underlying feeling or belief, and, in turn, to the kind of behavior that can help a couple meet their goal. If, for example, partners *believe* that they are responsible for their own behavior, and if they *feel* that their marriage can be satisfying, then they can demonstrate their belief by choosing behaviors that help them reach their goal of accepting responsibility. The central purpose of this book is to help couples develop skills—ways of behaving—that support the positive goals of marriage.

Relationship-destroying Goals

In many marriages individuals choose behaviors that create a chasm in their relationship, even though they want a greater sense of belonging and a feeling of importance. They may be unaware that they have chosen ineffective behaviors. When one or both partners have not learned behaviors that help them meet their goals of belonging and importance, they often become discouraged and behave in ways that further separate them from creating a satisfying relationship. For example, tears may be used to win arguments. Tears serve as water power to control, hurt, or gain special attention. "He's crying; I must have really hurt him. I'll take back everything." Anger may be used to make one partner conform to the other partner's wishes. "I better not do that or my wife will go berserk." Similarly, anger may be used to gain attention or to get a partner to listen. "He only listens when I become violent and throw things. Otherwise he's like a rock." Some individuals unknowingly use depression in order to get their partners to sit up and take notice, or to gain control. "I am depressed tonight. I don't see how I can go to the dinner party." A depressed mate can keep a partner from social events, recreation, or other responsibilities. The partner may even take over the depressed individual's responsibilities.

In marriages where these behaviors are common, the positive goals of marital behavior have inadvertently been replaced by negative goals that undermine a relationship. What are these relationship-destroying goals?

Rudolph Dreikurs discovered that behaviors chosen by discouraged persons are generally directed toward one of four goals: excusing oneself for shortcomings, attracting attention, gaining power, and vengeance.[5]

Excuse for shortcomings

When a person is unable to accept feelings of adequacy and holds no hope for success, the individual may choose to blame the marriage partner.

Attracting attention

A person who feels discouraged and inadequate may constantly seek attention and approval from the marriage partner. The person's sense of importance comes only from the attention of the partner.

Gaining power

An individual who feels unimportant and unfulfilled may choose to make unreasonable demands on the marriage partner and thereby to assert "I'm in control. I can do what I want."

If we feel unimportant, we may make unreasonable demands to assert "I'm in control."

Vengeance

If a person feels disliked, betrayed, or treated unfairly, and has given up all hope of being liked or accepted, the discouraged individual may choose to hurt the partner by word or deed.

When marriage partners have not learned to find a sense of belonging and importance in a positive fashion, they often become discouraged and their behavior is directed toward one of these four relationship-destroying goals. Most conflicts in marriage can be explained by identifying the relationship-destroying goals that the partners have knowingly or unknowingly chosen.

Some individuals promote conflict by being openly hostile, argumentative, and contradictory. Others exhibit passive destructive behaviors such as laziness, stubbornness, or forgetfulness. **Chart 1B** summarizes the four relationship-destroying goals, the underlying feelings or beliefs, and behaviors frequently chosen to meet each goal.

Chart 1B

Relationship-destroying Goals		
Goal	*Feelings/Beliefs*	*Behavior*
To excuse shortcomings.	Feelings of inadequacy. Has no hope for success.	Blames others for shortcomings.
To attract attention.	Feels important only when involved with partner. Feels inadequate and discouraged.	Seeks continuous signs of devotion from partner. Demands approval.
To gain power.	Feels ungratified. Needs to assert self in order to feel important and get necessary love and attention.	Makes unreasonable demands on partner in order to show control.
Vengeance.	Feels disliked, betrayed or treated unfairly. Has given up hope of being liked and accepted.	Hurts partner by word or deed—such as by bringing up past mistakes or issues where partner is most vulnerable.

Chart 1C

How to Identify a Relationship-destroying Goal			
Relationship-Destroying Goal	A. Behavior	B. Partner's Response	C. Consequence
To excuse shortcomings.	Blames others for shortcomings.	Feels frustrated, discouraged, or like giving up.	Resists taking responsibility. Increases attempts to blame.
To attract attention.	Seeks continuous signs of devotion. Demands approval.	Feels annoyed. "Can't you wait until I'm finished?"	Stops behavior, but only temporarily.
To gain power.	Makes unreasonable demands to show "I can do what I want; I'm in control!"	Feels challenged, angry, or argumentative. "You can't do this to me."	Continues or even intensifies destructive behavior.
Vengeance.	Hurts partner by word or deed.	Feels hurt and confused by what appears to be senseless hurting.	Hurts and punishes more to get even.

By learning to identify the goal of a partner's behavior, and the underlying feeling or belief, an individual can choose to respond in a way that will be helpful rather than harmful to the relationship.

How can you identify the goal of your partner?

A. Notice what your partner does.

B. Notice how you feel.

C. Be aware of what your partner does when you respond to his or her action.

Chart 1C will guide you in determining the goal of your marriage partner.

Whenever a relationship-destroying goal is identified, corrective action can be taken to replace the goal with a positive goal of marital behavior.

Goal	Corrective Action
To excuse shortcomings.	Do not criticize. Encourage partner to try alternative behaviors. Recognize positive attempts with hugs, kisses, and compliments. Be patient. Avoid self-discouragement.
To attract attention.	Ignore as much as possible. Acknowledge constructive and caring behavior. Use options and not demands when destructive behavior occurs.
To gain power.	Avoid power struggles by not attempting to win arguments. If you are becoming angry find a calmer time for discussion.
Vengeance.	Understand partner's motivation. Remain calm. Avoid retaliation and being hurt. Show partner he or she is loved and worthy. Respond to hurt with kindness. Communicate honestly.

The following examples will give you practice in identifying relationship-destroying goals.

Returning from a night of dancing, Susie suggests to Sam that she would like to stop for a snack. He agrees, and when they arrive at the restaurant he orders a rich, calorie-filled dessert. Susie admonishes him, "You don't need all those calories." Sam is hurt and thinks to himself, "Why does she always set me up like this?" When the food comes, he refuses to eat. Susie becomes irate and accuses him of wasting what little money they have.

Use **Chart 1C** to analyze the interaction between Sam and Susie.

A. What does Susie choose to do that upsets Sam?
Susie implies that Sam is overweight.

B. What is Sam's response?
Sam feels hurt and refuses to eat the food.

C. What does Susie do next?
Susie accuses Sam of wasting their money.

In **Chart 1C** we see that Susie is choosing a behavior of hurting Sam by attacking him in an area where he is most vulnerable. This interaction, then, appears to fit the goal of vengeance. The corrective action for Sam is to understand Susie's motivation, to remain calm, and to try not to hurt in return. This understanding can help him return love for hurt.

Tom is an avid sports fan. When he isn't playing the sport in season, he is perched in front of the television watching baseball, tennis, basketball, golf, or anything else sports related. Becky is fed up with Tom's preoccupation and now has begun to come into the room when he's watching television and demand that he stop watching whatever game is in progress. Tom responds by saying, "Yes, I'll stop watching in just a few minutes." But he goes right on watching. Tom's refusal to change makes Becky angrier and angrier. Finally, one Saturday afternoon Becky walks into the TV room with a piece of pie in her hand. She throws the pie in Tom's face and runs from the house screaming, "I'm going to leave you—you inconsiderate bum."

A. Becky demands that Tom stop watching sports events on television. We can assume that Tom's preoccupation with sports leaves little time for him to spend with Becky.

B. What is Tom's response? He says he'll stop watching "in a few minutes" but he doesn't. We can assume he had no intention of stopping.

C. How does Becky respond? Becky retaliates with anger and tells Tom she is leaving him.

This interaction seems to fit a goal of power. In a marriage relationship it is not always easy to determine which partner's behavior is actually doing more to destroy the relationship. When a goal of power is identified, either partner can help correct the problem by not attempting to win arguments, by not becoming angry and/or jealous, and by finding an alternative, calmer time to discuss the problem.

Gary annoys Laura with habits such as not entering in the check book the amounts of checks he writes, forgetting to drop off clothes at the cleaners on his way to work, not remembering to leave work early to pick up one of the children at a music lesson, etc. If Laura reminds him of what he needs to do, he is more likely to remember. But Laura sometimes feels she has another child to take care of. If Gary forgets to do something, he blames Laura for not reminding him at the right time. Laura is really frustrated. This has been going on for nine years!

What is Gary's goal? How could this goal be replaced by a positive goal? What corrective action could Laura take?

Paula is dedicated to her teaching career and is also very active in community groups. Rick has only recently become aware that for years he has felt rejected by Paula. He has shared his feelings of rejection with Paula, and she has made many attempts to spend more time with Rick. Rick seldom acknowledges her attempts, and when he does, he accuses her of being phoney. Paula feels confused and hurt.

What is Rick's goal? How could his goal be replaced by a positive goal?

There is always a choice in the way we respond. As a couple becomes aware of their choices, they can choose actions, thoughts, and words that support the positive goals of marriage. For every choice that potentially undermines a relationship there are alternative choices that support the positive goals. It is not the challenges that differ between successful and unsuccessful marriages but the choices couples make in meeting or avoiding the challenges.

The key to effective change of behavior is *learning to act rather than react.* Learn to catch yourself before you respond, to allow yourself to change from a reaction to a chosen action. As you become aware of how you might respond, pause briefly and then move ahead with a new response.

When we choose the positive goals of marriage, we can apply new skills that will help us to meet our goals of accepting responsibility, cooperating, contributing, and encouraging.

Planning for a Better Marriage

A healthy, satisfying marriage relationship is never accidental. Basic to the process of building a stronger, happier marriage is a commitment to spend time together learning and applying relationship skills. To improve your relationship, you may need to change your habitual ways of being with each other. Instead of spending leftover time together, you can learn to plan so that you have the time together that you need in order to place into action your commitment to build a better marriage. Planning will help you identify ways to change your day-to-day routine so that you can move toward reaching your goals.

Without planning, a couple may spend only leftover time together.

Planning and time management strategies are tools to put into use right now. Few people ever start out as good planners, but with practice everyone can develop these skills. Planning is a two-step process. First, you identify what you want to see happen in your marriage, and second, you establish your priorities. When you have established your priorities, you can begin to organize your time so that what you are choosing to do is compatible with priorities you have set.

Many of us confuse planning with a mental process that can more accurately be described as daydreaming. Writing your goals makes your planning more effective.

To give you practice in planning, make a list of your personal lifetime goals. Begin by asking yourself, *"What would I do if I had only one year to live?"* Write a list of activities that you want to accomplish. Write your list in the order that the items occur to you. When you finish writing decide which items are the most important. Alan Lakein developed the ABC Priority System, a method for identifying priorities.[6] Lakein's method will be useful to you in rating the items on your list. Place an *A* next to those items that you currently value the most, a *B* next to those items with medium value, and a *C* next to those with low value. Don't be overly concerned if you are unsure of the rankings. In general, the items you mark with an A will be those that you feel you will get the most satisfaction from doing; that is, they will yield the most value.

Are you currently spending time on activities that reflect your priorities? As you begin to plan your time more carefully, you can make certain that what you are choosing to do with your time is compatible with your priorities.

Now apply the same technique to the task of identifying the goals and priorities for your marriage. *What is it that you would like to see happen in your marriage?* Write a list of goals. To keep the task manageable, spend no more than 15 minutes. Use Lakein's ABC Priority System. Compare your priorities with your partner's priorities. *In what areas are you in general agreement? Are there major areas of conflict? Do you currently have many of the same goals? Are you spending time in activities that are related to the goals that are your priorities?*

Walter and Karen were in agreement regarding two A-level priorities: having a good marriage and spending time with each other. They also agreed that maintaining a clean house, yard, and car were C-level priorities. However, despite their mutual high rankings, they seldom found time to be together. On the other hand, their house, yard, and car were well maintained. With their new awareness of how they were actually spending their time, they learned to manage their time so that their actions were in harmony with their stated priorities.

To be effective, planning must be done on a regular basis. At different times you may have different priorities, individually and as a couple. When you know what your priorities are right now, you can find ways to support each other in meeting individual and marriage goals. The following time management skills will be helpful to you in your planning.

1. Establish written goals and objectives.
2. Review and revise your goals monthly.

At times a couple may disagree on priorities. It is important to align goals.

3. Each morning determine the priorities for the day.

4. Make time. There is always enough time for important things.

5. Do first things first.

6. Ask yourself, "What is the best use of my time right now?"

7. Enjoy whatever you are doing.

8. Build on successes.

9. Don't waste time regretting failures or feeling guilty.

Spending time together is an important behavior in a good marriage relationship. Begin now to plan time together. If you have not been spending regularly planned time together, the time may at first seem artificial. Eventually you will recognize that planned time is essential to your relationship.

Daily Dialogue

Put your planning and time management skills to work right now by finding time each day for one of the most important activities in your marriage—daily dialogue.

What is daily dialogue? Each day you will have a sharing time—a time in which you tell your partner what is going on with you right now. Set aside ten minutes a day for this important time together. Allow five minutes for each of you to share. This is a time for sharing feelings, not facts. When you share your feelings, you share your real self.

What do you share? Hopes and fears, excitement and anxiety, joy and sorrow, pride and embarrassment, apprehension, feelings of inadequacy, feelings of anger—in short, the important things that rarely are shared but are essential information for people who love each other.[7] Daily dialogue is *not* a time in which you ventilate or attempt to manipulate by making your partner feel responsible for your emotions. Daily dialogue is *not* a time for making demands or requests. As you practice daily dialogue you will learn to accept what your partner is saying and to share your feelings with greater ease. Give yourself time to

become accustomed to the process. It takes time to learn to share our deepest feelings. By giving you a deeper understanding and fuller acceptance of each other, dialogue breathes life into your marriage relationship.[8]

David Mace describes the value of daily dialogue in this way: "Without self-awareness, you are not in charge of your own life—it's as simple as that. And without other-awareness you don't know where your partner is, and in consequence you don't know when to comfort, when to support, when to praise, when to help—the very things loving people do for each other."[9]

Daily dialogue sets the stage for both encouragement meetings, which are discussed in Chapter 2, and marriage meetings, which are discussed in Chapter 6.

Marital Self-evaluation

To enrich your marriage it is helpful to assess your marriage satisfaction at this point in time. If you know where you are it is easier to sense where you want to go from here. Use the Marital Self-evaluation form found at the end of this chapter to honestly assess your marriage as you begin this program. Your assessment can be used for discussion with your partner or kept confidential. Keep in mind that in all marriages there are ups and downs.

We can compare couple relationships to gardens. Given daily attention, each brings pleasure. However, when neglected each requires enormous work to put back in order. As you proceed with your study, you will find that time together is essential to learning each of the skills that will enrich your marriage. Start now to make time together a high priority.

By accepting responsibility for your behavior, by seeking to identify your priorities, and by taking time to plan and to be together, you are demonstrating that you are committed to building the marriage relationship you really desire. You are using the tools at your disposal: time and effort.

References

1. Ken Cooper, *The Aerobics Program for Total Well-Being* (NY: Evans, 1982).

2. Gay Hendricks and Jon Carlson, *The Centered Athlete* (Englewood Cliffs, NJ: Prentice-Hall, 1982).

3. Lawrence LeShan, *How to Meditate* (NY: Bantam, 1975).

4. Jon Carlson, *The Basics of Stress Management* (Coral Springs, Florida: CMTI Press, 1982).

5. Rudolph Dreikurs, *The Challenge of Marriage* (NY: Hawthorn, 1949).

6. Alan Lakein, *How to Get Control of Your Time and Your Life* (NY: Signet Books, 1973).

7. David Mace, *Love and Anger in Marriage* (Grand Rapids, MI: Zondervan, 1982).

8. John Powell, *The Secret of Staying in Love* (Niles, IL: Argus Communications, 1974).

9. David Mace, *Love and Anger in Marriage*, p. 99.

Questions

1. The authors state, "A good marriage begins with you." Does one person have the power to change a relationship?

2. What does *the courage to be imperfect* do for a marriage?

3. How can self-discipline help your marriage relationship?

4. What are the goals of positive marital behavior?

5. There are three steps partners can use to identify relationship-destroying goals. How will you know if your partner is seeking attention? power? revenge? excusing shortcomings?

6. The authors state, "The key to effective change of behavior is *learning to act rather than react.*" What does this mean to you?

7. Why is spending planned time together essential in a marriage relationship?

8. Daily dialogue helps you become more aware of your partner and yourself. Why are self-awareness and other-awareness so important in a marriage relationship?

Activity for the Week

Each day this week take ten minutes for Daily Dialogue with your partner. The Daily Dialogue skill card will help you as you begin this process.

Complete the Marital Self-evaluation.

*Listen to "Relaxation" on *Time to Relax and Imagine*, your personal audiocassette.

Optional activity

To reinforce your understanding of goals:

a. Notice what you and your partner do that supports the positive goals of marriage. Share your observations with your partner.

b. In what ways do you or your partner seem to be working to achieve power, attention, vengeance, or to excuse shortcomings?

---

*The cassette, *Time to Relax and Imagine*, is available from American Guidance Service, Circle Pines, MN. An order form is provided in the back of this book.

1. The behaviors and skills necessary for an effective marriage are learned.

2. In order to love someone else, we must first love ourselves.

3. Most marriages can be improved when we understand ourselves and learn to behave differently.

4. Self-esteem is strengthened when we realize that we have control over our own lives.

5. We have the *power to choose* our beliefs, feelings, behaviors, and attitudes.

6. We can learn to act rather than react by catching ourselves before we respond and choosing a new response more in line with our positive goals.

7. All behavior is goal-directed. When you identify the goal of your behavior or your partner's behavior, you can better understand each other's actions.

8. In healthy marriages partners choose the following positive goals: to cooperate, to contribute, to encourage, and to accept responsibility for individual behavior.

9. Most marital conflict involves one of the following relationship-destroying goals: to excuse shortcomings, to gain power, to attract attention, or vengeance.

10. To identify your partner's goal:
a. Notice how you *feel* when your partner acts.
b. Be aware of what your partner *does* when you act to correct the behavior.

11. Planning and time management skills help us change our day-to-day routine so that we can move toward reaching our goals.

12. Planning helps us find time to be together, time for relaxation and physical fitness, and time to be alone—essential ingredients for personal and marital satisfaction.

MY ◆ PLAN

Ways I can encourage _____
_____

Strengths I can use to improve the relationship _____
_____

Ways I can show I care or appreciate _____
_____

Ways I can improve my communication _____
_____

Effective ways I can resolve conflict _____
_____

I am ready and willing to change my behavior in the following way(s): _____
_____

MY PROGRESS IN APPLYING THESE SKILLS	I am doing this more	I need to do this more	I remain about the same
Listening to feelings			
Communicating honestly			
Encouraging			
Daily dialogue			
Communicating love			
Encouragement meetings			
Marriage meetings			
Resolving conflict effectively			
Demonstrating specific caring behavior			
Choosing a better marriage			
Spending time with my partner			

MARITAL SELF-EVALUATION

Circle the number that reflects how you feel about each item below at this time:

POSITIVE   NEGATIVE

10	9	8	7	6	5	4	3	2	1

1. I understand my goals and my partner's goals. / I do not understand my goals and my partner's goals.

10	9	8	7	6	5	4	3	2	1

2. I encourage my partner. / I don't encourage my partner.

10	9	8	7	6	5	4	3	2	1

3. I listen to my partner. / I don't listen to my partner.

10	9	8	7	6	5	4	3	2	1

4. I recognize and understand my partner's feelings. / I don't recognize and understand my partner's feelings.

10	9	8	7	6	5	4	3	2	1

5. I can see the positive potential in situations. / I am pessimistic.

10	9	8	7	6	5	4	3	2	1

6. My communication with my partner is honest and open. / My communication is not open and honest.

10	9	8	7	6	5	4	3	2	1

7. I believe I am responsible for my own positive self-esteem. / I blame my partner and others for my lack of self-esteem.

10	9	8	7	6	5	4	3	2	1

8. I plan and communicate my intentions openly. / I fail to plan and communicate my intentions.

10	9	8	7	6	5	4	3	2	1

9. I recognize and choose my behavior and beliefs. / I am a victim of my behavior and beliefs.

10	9	8	7	6	5	4	3	2	1

10. I resolve conflict with my partner. / I try to get my way or prove I am right.

10	9	8	7	6	5	4	3	2	1

11. I spend enough quality time with my partner. / I spend little quality time with my partner.

10	9	8	7	6	5	4	3	2	1

12. We share marriage responsibilities in a fair manner. / We do not share marriage responsibilities.

10	9	8	7	6	5	4	3	2	1

13. We have fun in many different ways. / We do not know how to have fun.

Circle the number that represents your current level of satisfaction in each of the following areas:

1 = dissatisfied   5 = average satisfaction   10 = very satisfied

14. Work	1	2	3	4	5	6	7	8	9	10
15. Management of household chores	1	2	3	4	5	6	7	8	9	10
16. Social interaction with each other	1	2	3	4	5	6	7	8	9	10
17. Social interaction with other people	1	2	3	4	5	6	7	8	9	10
18. Demonstration of affection	1	2	3	4	5	6	7	8	9	10
19. Sexual relationship	1	2	3	4	5	6	7	8	9	10
20. Meaning of life and spirituality	1	2	3	4	5	6	7	8	9	10
21. Parenting	1	2	3	4	5	6	7	8	9	10
22. Leisure and recreation	1	2	3	4	5	6	7	8	9	10
23. Family finances	1	2	3	4	5	6	7	8	9	10
24. Time together (Quantity and quality)	1	2	3	4	5	6	7	8	9	10

Encouragement is a process that can be applied
in any situation.

Encouragement in the Marital Relationship

*E*ncouragement is the force that builds a happy marital relationship. What does it mean to encourage another person? By our words and actions we communicate to the person, "I accept you as you are, I understand your goals and desires, I value you," rather than "I accept you if . . . , I understand, but . . . , I value you unless . . . " Encouragement is unconditional love. It is given with no strings attached—no ifs, buts, or maybes. By encouraging, we allow each other the freedom to express thoughts and feelings without fearing rejection. We free each other to think our own thoughts, have our own feelings, and make our own decisions.

When our marriage doesn't meet our expectations, we become discouraged. Normal challenges begin to appear overwhelming. When one or both partners are discouraged, a marriage relationship is especially vulnerable. Discouragement can be replaced by encouragement. The process is challenging, and it requires time and patience.

In this chapter, you will learn the skills of encouragement and ways to apply the skills to your marriage. You will be able to put courage, joy, and hope into your relationship.

Characteristics of Encouragement

Encouragement should become a way of life in a marriage relationship. Encouragement is a process that can be applied in any situation. It is impossible to give too much encouragement! By accepting, valuing, and affirming your partner you exercise the most powerful positive skills available to you. Let's examine the characteristics of encouragement:

Acceptance

When we accept a person, we place no expectation on the person to improve or be different. We eliminate the pressure that subtly communicates, "Please me," or "Meet my standards." Acceptance is complete and unconditional, giving the person the freedom to choose to grow or to stay put. Given this option, the individual often chooses to move ahead. It should be noted, however, that if the person is chemically dependent or engaged in self-destructive behavior, professional help should be sought.

Showing Faith

We encourage each other by having confidence in each other. We choose to believe in our partner even though at times there may be little concrete evidence to support our faith. Our faith can be expressed aloud by saying "I know you are doing your best," "I believe in you," or silently by not pointing out the partner's limitations or faults. A smile and restraint from criticism are sufficient.

When you believe in someone, you trust the person to do what was promised. If a partner says, "I will be late because of a meeting," you show your faith by not calling to verify whereabouts. If you feel there are reasons to doubt your partner's word, take time for discussion.

Recognizing Effort

We communicate encouragement by recognizing and commenting on our partner's effort and improvement. Encouragement recognizes not only superior accomplishment, but any kind of positive movement. It is important to note effort as it occurs. Plan a time to recognize each other's efforts. By recognizing even small improvements and any positive changes, we provide the incentive to continue. Simple words that recognize the effort and credit the contribution are often all that is needed to sustain the effort. You might say, "I appreciated . . ." "I really enjoyed . . . Thanks!" "That really helped." Or, "That really took a load off of me."

Focusing on Strengths

Encouragement is a powerful tool in helping an individual become aware of strengths and resources. The ability to identify resources and skills in another is not unlike the ability to recognize potential in an athlete or a diamond in the rough. As an encouraging person, you identify undiscovered talent. As you communicate the strengths you observe, your partner will become more aware of personal assets.

If you feel unable to recognize and affirm your partner's strengths, this may be a reflection of your own feeling of inadequacy. Can you identify six or seven of your own strengths? You may say, for example, "I am energetic," "I have a purpose in life," "I enjoy helping," "I respect myself," etc. If you find the process of identifying your personal strengths difficult, you may not be practicing self-acceptance. You can learn to focus on your own positive actions and traits. As you understand and value yourself, you will find you are more easily able to identify strengths of your partner.

The process of self-affirmation will help you focus on your assets. Find a quiet time and place to practice self-affirmation. Relax your body by closing your eyes and taking deep breaths. Once you are relaxed, pick a quality that you want to possess. Visualize yourself with the quality. For example, you may want to be more patient, loving, or to enjoy other people more. After visualizing yourself with the quality, see your partner with you, telling you that you are loving, or patient, etc. By practicing self-affirmation, you will allow the meaning of the statement to become a part of you.

By identifying your own strengths and by practicing self-affirmation, you will more easily recognize the assets and strengths of your partner. Take time to make a list of your partner's strengths.

As partners learn to affirm each other's resources, there is an increase in self-esteem for each person. The marriage relationship is strengthened, giving the couple the feeling of togetherness they desire.

Why Does A Person Become Discouraged?

Although we all experience feelings of disappointment or discouragement from time to time, the person who is continually discouraged may be responding to mistaken ideas about human relationships. As a result, for this individual life just isn't what it is supposed to be. Negative ideas or concepts that contribute to discouragement include the following:

1. "I must be loved and approved by everyone for everything I do at all times." For this individual, every decision and action must bring approval. When the expected approval does not come, the person feels rejected.

Frequently our behavior towards each other has a discouraging effect.

2. "Things must go the way I want them to go or it is awful." For this person, it is crucial that any difference of opinion is resolved in his or her own way. When challenged, the person becomes angry and agitated.

3. "My partner *makes* me unhappy." This individual does not understand that happiness and unhappiness are feelings that we generate internally. No one is to blame for our unhappiness.

4. "My partner should be happy to take care of me." This person insists on being taken care of and believes that the partner should be pleased to have the privilege.

5. "There is always one right, perfect, and precise solution, and it is a calamity if it is not found." This individual seeks the perfect job, the perfect friendship, the perfect vacation, etc., and because perfection isn't obtainable, remains discouraged.

6. "The world should be fair." This individual operates from a belief that is fiction. Faced with the many inequities in life, the person continuously battles against reality.

When a person operates from these mistaken beliefs, there is continual disappointment and discouragement, and resulting low self-esteem. No one is loved and approved by everyone. We can't always get our way. Sometimes life is unfair. There are no perfect solutions.

Discouraged partners feel inadequate, inept, and powerless to do anything about their situations. Because discouraged partners view their situations as hopeless, they act on that belief. As a result, their actions become self-defeating.

> Connie believes that other people do not like her. When she is at a party she is cautious about approaching people, and she moves away quickly if they don't respond. People think of her as aloof. Thus, her belief helps encourage the response that she wants to avoid.

The beliefs and expectations we create in our marriage relationship are powerful. Often we operate on the basis of what we feel our partners should do rather than what they are doing. As a result we frequently focus on faults rather than virtues. Whether we label their actions faults or strengths depends on our attitude and our priorities.

If our priority is to feel inadequate, or to feel we are a victim, any encouragement we receive from our partner is discounted. Eventually our partner ceases trying to encourage.

Unreasonable standards lead to discouragement.

If our priority is to please others, we strive to avoid rejection. When we believe that everyone else must be pleased at all costs, we forget our own needs and neglect to value ourselves.

If our priority is to control, we continually guard against humiliation and put-downs, which naturally reduces our spontaneity. We may attempt to maintain control by calling attention to our partner's faults.

If our priority is perfectionism, or superiority, we have little tolerance for mistakes, and we compulsively monitor ourselves and our partner. Our expertise in fault-finding causes our partner to feel inadequate.

These priorities separate us from our goal of belonging and togetherness. However, there are potential assets that can be found if we shift our focus. The person whose priority is to control can also be recognized as an individual with the potential to lead, to organize, and to be productive. In the individual whose priority is to please others, we can see the potential assets of friendliness, consideration, and flexibility. For the individual whose priority is perfectionism, or superiority, there is the potential for assuming responsibility, ambition, courage, and the ability to find meaning in everything. The individual whose priority is to feel victimized has the potential for empathy and helpfulness.

How Do We Discourage Each Other?

Although we may have good intentions, frequently our behavior toward each other has a discouraging effect. Let's examine four common methods of discouragement: subtle domination, intimidation, failing to acknowledge progress, and oversensitivity.

Subtle Domination Sometimes we feel that our way is the best and only way of accomplishing something. In order to have the job "done right," we choose to take over the job rather than to be satisfied with our partner's progress. Although our intention may be good, we are practicing subtle domination. The act of dominating, no matter how subtle, communicates rejection and discourages our partner. Areas in which we may be practicing subtle domination include cleanliness and care of the home, painting, shopping, accounting and paying bills, supervising the children, and making social arrangements. Are your perfectionistic standards in any of these areas resulting in discouragement for your partner?

Intimidation If we continually expect our partner to be more and do more, our partner realizes that no matter what is accomplished, it will not meet our standards. Like subtle domination, intimidation communicates rejection and leads to discouragement. This may lead to depression, and, in some marriages, the partner may consider divorce.

> Oralee expects Dave to get regular salary increases at work and also to plan a sparkling social life. If either of these expectations is not realized, Oralee is very upset. She immediately compares Dave with other men she knows. Dave reacts by spending excessive time away from home, becoming more and more involved with his own interests. Dave believes, "No matter what I do, I can never please Oralee."

Oversensitivity If we operate from the faulty assumption that "I am only something if I am more than others," we may feel the need to attack what is perceived as a threat to our imagined superiority. For example, if a partner mentions how well dressed another husband or wife appeared, how enjoyable a meal was, or how openly affection was expressed, the oversensitive partner interprets the comments as a put-down, and strikes out in anger. Eventually this oversensitive behavior influences sharing and risk-taking within the marriage. The partner learns that whatever is said will be heard in a different way than is intended. As a result, the partner becomes cautious in order to avoid the oversensitive reaction.

Failing to Acknowledge Progress By failing to recognize progress, we practice another subtle form of discouragement. Our silence prevents our partner from getting positive feedback that could provide the motivation to keep trying. Like subtle domination, failing to recognize progress communicates rejection.

For example, when a partner is trying to lose weight, it is discouraging to point out occasional overeating. It is more helpful to note successes. Instead of saying, "That bread is not on your diet," a more encouraging remark would be, "I know it is challenging to be on a diet, and you are following through most of the time. I can see the progress you are making."

Encouragement Skills

We have examined some common factors that bring discouragement to a marriage relationship. Even though our intentions may be good, whenever we subtly dominate, intimidate, are oversensitive, or fail to acknowledge progress, we discourage our partners. How can we replace discouragement with encouragement?

As you become more aware of the positive qualities and behaviors in each other, it is important to communicate what you feel and observe about each other. In your marriage relationship you can provide encouragement by using the following skills:

Listening

The encouraging listener hears not only words but also feelings behind the words. To listen effectively, we must be totally in the present. This means that we focus our attention on what is being said rather than allow ourselves to be distracted by the television, the newspaper, the children's behavior, or an idea we are waiting to express. We listen so that we are able to identify the theme or central idea of our partner's words. We listen in order to focus on a possible encouraging response. Here are two exercises that illustrate listening skills:

> Your partner says, "I'm sick and tired of what they are doing to me at work. It's not fair. I'm not going to take it any more!"
>
> *What is the theme or central idea being expressed; that is, what is it your partner believes?*
>
> *Were you able to identify that your partner believes he or she is not treated fairly and intends to do something about it? What can you do to encourage your partner?*
>
> Your partner says, "That's the last straw. They're having a party at the Smith's. It seems like everyone is invited except us."
>
> *What does your partner believe?*
> *How can you encourage your partner?*

As you learn to listen for the belief and feeling, you can respond in an encouraging way.

To listen effectively, we must be totally in the present.

Responding With Empathy

Empathy is the ability to enter another person's world and understand how that person feels. When we respond empathetically, we demonstrate that we understand the feelings and the theme being expressed. This does not necessarily mean that we agree. We listen carefully in order to see the situation through the other person's eyes. Then we choose to respond in a way that shows we have heard and understand. In the following examples, identify the belief and the feeling. Then think of a way to respond with empathy.

> Your partner comes home from work and says, "They're really tightening things up at the plant. I get the feeling that they may be thinking they'll have to let me go rather than put me back on the assembly line. Maybe they think I can't handle the work because of my disability."
>
> *What is the feeling?*
> *What is the belief?*
> *How can you respond with empathy?*

You come home from work and your partner says, "The kids have been hellions all day. As soon as I start something, one of the kids has a request. I just can't accomplish anything."

What is the feeling?
How can you respond with empathy?

We may unknowingly have learned a way of responding that is discouraging rather than encouraging. What are some common response styles that lead to discouragement? Talking as a superior to an inferior, moralizing, intellectualizing, judging, or criticizing. The following exercise will help you discover whether your typical way of responding is discouraging or encouraging. Respond to these statements in your natural style. Then consider whether there is a more empathic way to respond.

"It just isn't fair! You expect us to entertain your relatives every holiday, and when they come you act like they're not even here. I feel like I never get a minute to myself."

Your natural response:_____

_____

A more empathic response:_____

_____

"I'm doing the best I can to stay within our budget, but you don't control your spending. Your new car is a good example of why our budget is never balanced."

Your natural response:_____

_____

A more empathic response:_____

_____

"Since your sister moved back to town, you're always on the phone. And she spends every Saturday with us. I feel like we never have any time alone."

Your natural response:_____

_____

A more empathic response:_____

_____

Do you hear your partner's complaints as an attack on you? If so, your response may be to defend yourself by attacking in return. To respond empathetically you will need a new orientation. Listen for the feelings and belief, and respond so that your partner knows you understand.

Communicating Respect

When we communicate respect, we encourage. By respecting your partner's unique and irreplaceable value as a human being, you provide support and hope that help build self-esteem. A discouraged partner often feels powerless to change a situation. By communicating respect, you say to your partner, "I know you have the ability to handle this situation. I know you will make good decisions. I trust you. I have faith in you."

Here are situations that require the ability to communicate respect. Think about how you would deal with each.

Your partner has just come home from a business meeting. He has been asked to accept a position with greater responsibility. You recognize that you may have to relocate for the second time in five years.

How can you communicate respect?
What would you say?
What would you do?

Your partner comes home discouraged and dejected. She has lost her biggest account and realizes this will reduce her income significantly. Your mutual plans for early retirement will be severely affected.

What do you say?
What do you do?

Sometimes we try to help by solving our partner's problem when support is what is really needed. Believing in your partner's ability to handle the situation is powerful encouragement. Some people are helped most by being permitted to deal with the problem in their own way. They may need only our support and faith in their ability to handle the situation.

Being Enthusiastic and Hopeful

When we express enthusiasm, we raise the spirits of those around us. Through our enthusiasm, we transmit positive energy. How do we express enthusiasm in our marriage? We can begin by learning to identify what is positive in our relationship. If you have been discouraged about your marriage, focus on the positive fact that you are becoming aware of what you want to change in your relationship. Look for something positive every day. As you search for the positive, you will find it! Communicate something positive every day. Act upon your positive impulses. If you feel an inclination to pick up a gift, give a hug, or make a surprise call, do it. Expect your partner to have positive intentions. By your positive expectations and by your positive manner and attitude, you encourage positive behavior.

Creating Positive Meanings and Alternatives

There are many ways to view any given situation. Each of us understands a situation from our own point of view. Therefore, it is always possible to choose another viewpoint. If there are situations in our marriages that we have considered negative, we can find a new way of viewing those situations. We can create positive meanings and alternatives. The following examples illustrate the process of finding a positive alternative way of regarding the situation.

Your partner gets up early to exercise before going to work. You are disturbed by the noise. You feel it is unfair and inconsiderate.

What is an alternative way of looking at this behavior? An alternative is to be pleased that your partner is maintaining physical fitness.

Your partner leaves early for work without waking you and telling you goodbye. You feel slighted and ignored.

What is an alternative way of looking at this behavior? An alternative is to recognize that your partner is being considerate and letting you sleep a few extra minutes.

Your wife calls from her parents' house out-of-town indicating she won't be home

There are many ways to view any given situation.

tomorrow as anticipated. There are a number of financial matters that have to be handled, and she wants to get them finalized before leaving.

If you look at this in a discouraging way, you will conclude that your feelings are not being considered. An encouraging alternative is to recognize your wife's thoughtfulness in calling you and in being willing to help her parents.

Your partner comes home from work deeply discouraged. The school district has to cut thirty-five teaching jobs, and she has low seniority. Your plans to take a vacation this summer will have to be put aside because you can't spend the money until she's sure of a job.

What positive alternative do you see in this situation? Your wife might have the opportunity to look into other career possibilities that have always interested her while she's waiting to see if the district will need her in the fall.

You always have an option about what you choose to see in any given situation. You create your own experiences. The situation itself does not directly cause a feeling. Rather, it is the meaning you give to the situation that influences your feelings. When you begin to see that you always have the opportunity to create a positive alternative, your marriage relationship will be enriched.

We often get in the habit of viewing certain traits in our partners as negative. As you learn to create positive alternatives, you can find a positive way of viewing these traits. For practice, identify a positive alternative way of regarding each of the traits below.

Trait Considered Negative	Alternative Positive View
Overly talkative	*Friendly*
Argumentative	*Loves a good discussion*
Demanding, forceful	
Conservative	
Liberal	
Complaining	
Quiet	
Show-off	

Now make a list of your partner's traits that you have considered negative. *What is an alternative way of regarding each of these traits?*

Encouraging Self

By encouraging yourself, you increase your sense of personal worth. In order to be a resource to others, it is important to develop self-esteem. Your self-esteem will grow as you learn to identify, verbalize, and own your personal strengths. Get rid of your fear of failure by not embracing it, holding on to it, or using it as an excuse to avoid positive movement. Learn to discover your hidden potential. Compliment yourself. Be sure the messages you are giving yourself are positive messages, such as "I am a good friend. People like me. My opinion is important. Others count on me."

The Encouragement Meeting

There are unlimited opportunities for encouraging each other. As you practice the skills of encouragement, you will identify numerous opportunities. Your encouragement will be a spontaneous response, demonstrating your caring. You may want to read *The Encouragement Book* by Don Dinkmeyer and Lewis Losoncy[1] and *The Basics of Encouragement* by Gary McKay[2] to give you additional ideas.

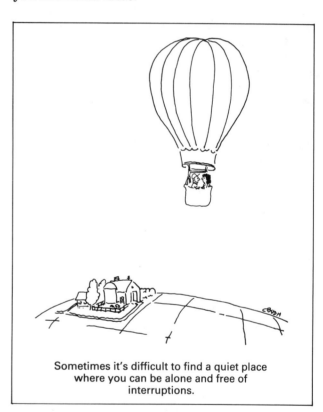

Sometimes it's difficult to find a quiet place where you can be alone and free of interruptions.

In addition to the spontaneous encouragement you share, planning time for encouragement will assure that you have the opportunity to nourish your relationship. Encouragement meetings provide a regular, systematic way to strengthen your marriage by focusing on what is positive. Schedule an encouragement meeting two or three times a week. Some couples so enjoy the process that they schedule daily meetings. The purpose of the encouragement meeting is to allow each person to share the positive things they are seeing in each other and in the relationship. The encouragement meeting has the following guidelines:

1. Meet in a place and at a time that is quiet and free of interruption.
2. Sit facing each other, close enough to hold hands comfortably.
3. One partner begins by saying, "The most positive thing that happened today was . . ." Then, the partner continues by saying, "Something I appreciated about you today was. . . ."
4. The partner who speaks first takes 3-5 minutes. The listening partner maintains eye contact to indicate attentiveness and does not interrupt. At the end of 3-5 minutes, the listening partner briefly feeds back the ideas, beliefs, feelings, or values heard, taking care not to challenge.
5. After the partner has given feedback, the process is repeated, with the other partner using the same sentences, "The most positive thing that happened today was . . .," followed by "Something I appreciated about you today was. . . ." The listening partner provides feedback.

When you are comfortable with this simple encouragement meeting format, additional topics may be used, such as

"The most enjoyable thing I did this week . . ."
"Something I enjoy about you is . . ."
"Something enjoyable I'm looking forward to doing with you is . . ."

The encouragement meeting nourishes a marriage relationship by focusing on what is positive. Through the process of identifying your own strengths and things to appreciate about your partner, each of you will experience greater self-esteem and greater respect for your marriage relationship.

Marriages in which encouragement is practiced are characterized by greater cooperation. When a couple is concerned about supporting each other and building mutual self-esteem, tendencies to compete with each other or to struggle for power are replaced by the desire to work together to achieve a sense of belonging and togetherness.

References

1. Don Dinkmeyer and Lewis Losoncy, *The Encouragement Book: Becoming a Positive Person* (Englewood Cliffs, NJ: Prentice-Hall, 1980).
2. Gary D. McKay, *The Basics of Encouragement* (CMTI Press, Box 8268, Coral Springs, FL, 1976.)

Questions

1. What does encouragement mean to you?
2. What are some basic characteristics of people who encourage?
3. What ideas or concepts contribute to a person's becoming discouraged?
4. What are some ways we discourage each other?
5. How can you listen in an encouraging manner?
6. The authors state, "You always have an option about what you choose to see in a given situation." What have you regarded as negative in your marriage? What is another positive way of looking at this aspect of your relationship?
7. Why is it important to encourage yourself? What are some specific ways you can encourage yourself?
8. What are the guidelines for the encouragement meeting?

Activity for the Week

Continue Daily Dialogue.

Hold an Encouragement Meeting three times this week. Focus on what you appreciate about your partner and what is positive in your relationship. The key topics may be:

"The most positive thing that happened today was . . ."

"Something I appreciate about you today is . . ."

When your partner encourages you in some way, let your partner know of your appreciation.

Begin Encouraging Days this week. Use the skill card, Encouraging Days, to guide you. Strive to do two encouraging behaviors each day.

Listen to "Self-Encouragement" on *Time to Relax and Imagine*, your personal audiocassette.*

---

*The cassette, *Time to Relax and Imagine*, is available from American Guidance Service, Circle Pines, MN. An order form is provided in the back of this book.

1. Encouragement is an essential force in building a happy marital relationship.

2. When you encourage your partner you show faith and confidence.

3. Encouragement recognizes small or large efforts and contributions.

4. Encouragers recognize resources and potential in their partners.

5. Listening and showing empathy are essential encouragement skills.

6. Domination, intimidation, oversensitivity, and failing to acknowledge progress cause discouragement.

7. We can learn to encourage ourselves and others by finding a positive way of viewing a discouraging situation.

8. Encouragement meetings provide a regular, systematic way to strengthen your marriage.

MY ◆ PLAN

Ways I can encourage _____
_____

Strengths I can use to improve the relationship _____
_____

Ways I can show I care or appreciate _____
_____

Ways I can improve my communication _____
_____

Effective ways I can resolve conflict _____
_____

I am ready and willing to change my behavior in the following way(s): ____
_____

MY PROGRESS IN APPLYING THESE SKILLS	I am doing this more	I need to do this more	I remain about the same
Listening to feelings			
Communicating honestly			
Encouraging			
Daily dialogue			
Communicating love			
Encouragement meetings			
Marriage meetings			
Resolving conflict effectively			
Demonstrating specific caring behavior			
Choosing a better marriage			
Spending time with my partner			

Marriage partners may unconsciously try to replicate
the environment they grew up in.

CHAPTER THREE

Understanding Your Relationship

Your marriage is your most important relationship. However, you may not be getting the most from this relationship because of a lack of understanding of factors that have a major influence on your relationship.

Like all relationships, your marriage has a system. Your marriage system reflects your personal goals, beliefs, and priorities, and the goals, priorities, and beliefs you share as a couple. If your goals and priorities are aligned, your marriage system functions smoothly. When you develop an understanding of your marriage system, you can learn to relate in an increasingly positive manner and assure that your goals and priorities are in harmony.

What you originally learned about how to relate to people was learned from your family. You observed cooperation, quarreling, getting even, love, and many other interactions. Observing your parents' marriage may not always be the best training for relating in your marriage, however. And even though you may each have come from a healthy, happy home environment, the systems operating in your respective homes may have been quite different. You may each try consciously or unconsciously to replicate the kind of environment that you are familiar with.

In this chapter you will learn about how your life style is formed, and how it affects your marriage relationship. When a couple's individual life styles contain conflicting priorities, a competitive atmosphere may result. Rather than openly communicating, the couple may resort to patterns of communication that are played like games, to be won or lost. You will learn to identify the games you play. This will free you to find alternative ways of behaving that will allow each of you to meet your needs.

In game terminology, your new behavior will allow each of you to win.

Life Style

Our life style provides guidelines for our actions and responses. The factors that form our life style are our beliefs, values, intentions or goals, perceptions, and priorities.

BELIEFS serve as guidelines in our relationships. You may have one or more basic beliefs such as, "I must be first," "I must be in control," "I must avoid stress," "I must please," "I must be right," etc.

VALUES are our opinions of what is most important to us.

INTENTIONS OR GOALS give direction and purpose to our relationship. Our goals may be expressions of our positive desire for cooperation, or they may be goals that separate us from each other—attention, power, revenge, and excusing shortcomings.

PERCEPTIONS are subjective meanings we give to events. We operate on the basis of how things seem to be. Our behavior is a result of our perception.

PRIORITIES are shorthand statements of our convictions. Our priorities answer the questions, "What is most important in my search for belonging and acceptance?" "What must I most urgently avoid?"

Understanding Your True Values

Values are an important part of our life style. Our values are sometimes deceptive. For example, we may *say* that we value a particular activity, but we do not *invest* ourselves in pursuing the activity. Here is an exercise to help you clarify your real values. The exercise was developed by Sidney Simon, Leland Howe, and Howard Kirschenbaum.[1]

List the twenty things you like to do the most. Write them in the order they occur to you. When you have completed the list, do the following:

$—Put a dollar sign next to each item that costs over five dollars every time you do it.

P/A—Place a P next to each item that you enjoy more when you are doing it with your partner. Place an A by items that you enjoy doing alone.

PL—Place PL next to each activity that requires planning.

S—Put an S next to each item you would want your partner to have on his or her list.

N/5—Put N/5 next to any item that would not have appeared on your list five years ago.

DATE—Beside each activity, place the date when you last did it.

When you have completed the exercise, write several statements about what you have learned about your real values. *Are you now choosing to invest your time, money, and energy in areas that you say are important to you?*

Life Style Types

The characteristic way you behave is a reflection of your subjective view of life, or life style. Although we are all unique, psychologists have found that we tend to express one dominant personality theme. For example, Karen Horney suggests that a person has a tendency to move toward others, to move away from others, or to move against others.[2]

People who move toward others want to be thought of as lovable. Because they want to avoid displeasing, they often find it difficult to assert themselves, to say no, or to express anger. To meet their goal of being loved, they tend to be self-sacrificing and helpful.

People who move against others need to be powerful, even if it means being feared. They assert themselves to excess. Their arrogance covers up their feelings of inadequacy and fears. They tend to be perfectionistic, demanding people.

People who move away from people value personal freedom above all else. They avoid commitments and can be described by words such as detached, aloof, and reserved. They regard themselves as independent, strong, and superior.

In our marriage relationship we each act out our basic personality theme, which may or may not mesh with our partner's personality theme. For example, if we tend to move toward people and our partner tends to move away from people, we may not find the closeness we need in the one case, or the independence we need in the other.

Harold Mosak and Bernard Shulman of the Alfred Adler Institute of Chicago identified life style types.[3] Like Horney's personality themes, these life style types describe common subjective views of life. The terms they adopted are particularly useful because they suggest the behavior associated with the life style.

1. **The Getter.** The Getter is solely concerned with self. "What's in it for me?" is the question on the Getter's mind. Getters are uncooperative, manipulative people who use whatever works—anger, charm, shyness—to put others into their service. The Getter operates from the belief that life is unfair and tends to lack self-reliance.

2. **The Controller.** "Control life so it doesn't control you" is the operating rule for the Controller. Controllers tend to be perfectionistic. Controllers commonly intellectualize and avoid sharing feelings. Controllers lack spontaneity.

3. **The Need to be Right.** A compulsion to know the right or wrong way to do everything guides these individuals' lives. Until they think they know what is "right" they are immobilized. Any mistakes are blamed on others.

4. **The Pleaser.** The Pleaser needs constant praise and reassurance. The need for approval diminishes the Pleaser's ability to be open and honest. Pleasers are overly sensitive to criticism.

5. **The Good One.** No one can live up to the standards of the Good One. The Good One is a self-

" THE CONTROLLER "

"Control life so it doesn't control you" is the operating rule for the Controller.

9. **The Aginner.** The Aginner finds little in life to support and much to be against. The Aginner is a complainer.

10. **The Computer.** The Computer avoids feelings at all costs. Problems can be solved by reason alone is the Computer's belief.

Our life style affects every relationship. When one person needs to be right, someone by implication is going to be wrong. If a person has a constant need to receive, someone is going to be in the position of always having to give. If someone believes reason is the only way to solve problems, someone else must keep his or her feelings undercover. Unfortunately, when our individual life styles are in conflict our marriage may become a competitive relationship rather than a supportive, cooperative relationship.

It is important to note that no one totally conforms to one life style description. At different times we may be expressing a different subjective view of life. This suggests that there is sometimes conflict within us regarding what we believe to be important. This also is a reflection of how our life style may change.

Family Atmosphere

The life style we bring to our marriage relationship is often a reflection of the family atmosphere in which we were raised. The family atmosphere is the climate of relationship in the home. It is the characteristic pattern the parents present to their children as a standard or guideline for human relationships. The values the parents share are generally adopted as values by their children. What the children enjoy doing subsequently reflects those shared values. For example, musical interests, athletic interests, or love of reading may result from shared family values. On the other hand, children may accept or reject values in areas in which there is competition between the parents.

Some family atmospheres are characterized by rigidity or impossible standards. More compliant children, in response, may accept the standards, and the standards become a part of their life style. Rebellious children may reject the standards. In either event, the children may end up with a subjective view of life, or life style, which hampers

righteous person, skilled at pointing out the weaknesses of others. The feelings and opinions of the Good One always are more important than anyone else's feelings or opinions. No one can live up to the standards of the Good One. When the Good One marries, the discouraged partner—who never can be good enough—may play out the role of the "bad" one by turning to alcohol, drugs, sexual promiscuity, or other "bad" behavior.

6. **The Victim.** For the Victim, life is full of gloom and doom. Victims chase disaster and set themselves up for disaster. Victims always see the pessimistic side of life.

7. **The Martyr.** Martyrs nobly suffer through life's injustices. But unlike the Victim, the Martyr—endowed with high moral standards—suffers for a "good cause." Martyrs are "injustice collectors" who keep track of how they have been treated unfairly and who has treated them unfairly.

8. **The Inadequate Person.** "Don't expect anything of me, please" is the plea of the inadequate person. People who feel inadequate are unable to meet the challenges of life. They avoid demands and pressures.

their adult relationships. However, as individuals become more aware of their perceptions and of their goals, they can choose new goals and behaviors that allow them to have the type of relationship they desire.

Which family atmospheres tend to foster competition and unsatisfying relationships? Some characteristic family atmospheres are described below.[4]

The REJECTIVE atmosphere is exemplified by parents who fail to separate the deed from the doer and who constantly criticize and reject their children.

The AUTHORITARIAN atmosphere is rigid, stresses obedience, and is likely to produce either extremely conforming or extremely rebellious children.

In the INCONSISTENT atmosphere, the children don't know what to expect of others or what is expected of them. However, most of the time in such an atmosphere it is the adults rather than the children who are confused.

The SUPPRESSIVE atmosphere limits the freedom to express thoughts and feelings and sometimes stimulates excessive daydreaming or produces children who are very good at putting up a front. Examples of this kind of atmosphere include the family made up of humorless people or a family with very narrow-minded attitudes concerning what is acceptable or unacceptable behavior.

The OVERPROTECTIVE atmosphere denies children the opportunity to learn to be responsible for their own behavior.

The HIGH STANDARDS atmosphere leads the children to feel that they are never good enough.

Family atmospheres that are more productive, supportive, and growth-stimulating are characterized by traits that are the opposite of traits found in the atmospheres described above. Supportive family atmospheres allow encouragement for each member of the family. Such atmospheres focus on the positive elements in the family relationship, are flexible, and emphasize equality and cooperation. The parents are consistent, allowing children to know what to expect, but they are not rigid. Productive atmospheres encourage open expression of thoughts, feelings, and intentions. Family members learn to be responsible for their own behavior. Rather than invoking high standards, the atmosphere is one of acceptance and encouragement.

We did not choose our family atmosphere as children, but we can create a family atmosphere now that is productive, supportive, and growth-stimulating. The first step in reshaping our family atmosphere is to identify as a couple whether our priorities allow us to focus on cooperation. When a marriage is characterized by conflict, one or both partners may be inadvertently focusing energy on meeting individual priorities rather than on meeting a mutual priority of cooperation.

Understanding our priorities is the key to understanding our marriage relationship. Let's examine common priorities that guide our behavior as individuals.

The Four Priorities of Life Style

Our individual priority answers the questions: "What is most important in my search for belonging and acceptance?" and "What must I most urgently avoid?" When we identify our priority we are better able to understand how our personality theme influences our marriage relationship. The priority, in a sense, reveals our personality theme in a shorthand fashion. The four priorities of life style are:

1. Control
2. Superiority
3. Pleasing
4. Comfort Seeking

We tend to have one dominant priority at a given time, although our personality style as a whole has varied proportions of each priority. Our priority is a guideline for us at this point in time. Our priority stimulates behavior that is in line with our goals. Priorities change as beliefs, goals, attitudes, and values change.

THE CONTROLLER. The priority of the Controller is to control self, the partner, and the relationship. This goal of power and control is accomplished through autocratic behavior or passive manipulation. Creativity and spontaneity are absent from the Controller's life. The Controller has few friends, and feels lonely and distant from people. The Controller seeks to avoid humiliation at all costs. The potential assets of the Controller are leadership, planning, and productivity. The partner whose priority is to control helps the marital relationship by taking a leadership role and developing contacts. This partner is good at planning and can be counted on to be productive and persistent.

THE SUPERIOR ONE. The priority of the Superior One is to be better than others. Feeling unequal to others, Superior Ones attempt to overcompensate, believing this will make them worthwhile. They strive to be more competent, more effective, more recognized, and more useful than others. Superior Ones seek to avoid meaninglessness and lack of purpose in all their activities. Consequently, they pay the price of feeling overburdened and over responsible. The potential assets of the Superior One include responsibility, ambition, courage, and perceptiveness. The partner of this courageous, ambitious person can find life exciting, though demanding.

"THE SUPERIOR ONE"

The Superior One strives to be more competent, more effective, more recognized, and more useful than others.

THE COMFORT SEEKER. The priority of the Comfort Seeker is pleasure. The Comfort Seeker's basic needs for love and affection were not met in early life. To compensate for this early life deficiency the Comfort Seeker becomes a spoiled brat. Comfort Seekers do not use their talents fully, and they tend to be unproductive, avoiding stress and responsibility at all costs. Comfort Seekers have the potential for being easy-going, undemanding, peace-making, flexible, and empathic. If their partners do not pressure them to improve, Comfort Seekers are easy to get along with, considerate, and good companions.

"THE COMFORT SEEKER"

The priority of the Comfort Seeker is pleasure.

THE PLEASER. The priority of the Pleaser is approval from others. The Pleaser believes that life is meaningful only if others frequently give their approval. Pleasers bend over backwards for others, operating on a please or perish basis. Pleasers feel alienated from people, and they lack respect for themselves and others. By continuously striving to avoid rejection, Pleasers pay the price of reduced personal growth. Pleasers make contact with others easily, are friendly, perceptive, and non-confrontive. However, because the Pleaser expects constant approval, the partner can become frustrated by the incessant need for approval and recognition.

If you are able to identify your priority, then you can ask yourself three questions:

If this is my priority, what am I trying to avoid?
What price am I paying as a result of having this priority?
What issue will dominate our relationship as long as I maintain this priority?

The following chart will help you answer these questions.

As you understand your own priorities you can become more aware of what you seek to avoid and the issue or feeling that the priority creates in your relationship. We pay a price to maintain a priority. Consider how a priority interferes with your relationship. As you become more aware you can learn to choose priorities that strengthen your relationship and, therefore, are mutually beneficial to you and your partner. You can choose to lead rather than overpower. You can choose to be a peacemaker so that each of you is more comfortable. You can learn to negotiate and compromise so that both you and your partner feel satisfied.

Games

When marriage partners struggle for control, they are focusing on personal gain rather than on growth of the relationship. To reach their goal, they adopt sophisticated, patterned maneuvers that are, in fact, destructive games. When marriage partners become aware of the non-constructive games they use, they can choose to develop a game-free, honest relationship.

Eric Berne was one of the first to popularize the idea of games people play.[5] The concept of games presented in this book is an adaptation of the games concept of Gerald Mozdzierz and Thomas Lottman[6] and is similar to Berne's concept.

When we are interested in our own status and dominance rather than in common goals, we may engage in games to gain superiority over our partners. As we learn to identify the games we play in our marriage relationship, we can understand more fully how our game-like behavior promotes conflict. Not all marital conflict can be understood in terms of games, but games do make us aware of methods we commonly use in our struggle for personal prestige or domination. As you become aware of the games you play, you may choose to

Chart 3A

Understanding My Priority			
My Priority	*What I Am Avoiding*	*The Price I Pay*	*The Issue*
Control	Embarrassment and humiliation.	Social distance; being overburdened.	Who is in charge?
Superiority	Meaninglessness; worthlessness.	Social distance.	Who is *more* correct?
Comfort	Stress or pain.	Reduced productivity.	Am I avoiding stress? Am I comfortable?
Pleasing	Rejection.	Reduced growth.	Am I pleasing you? Will they approve of me?

replace the games with communication that allows a more honest relationship in which you work together to find constructive, mutually satisfying solutions to conflict.

Each couple develops its own games and corresponding rules. As you read the descriptions that follow, decide whether these are games that you have observed, initiated, or participated in.

" THE PLEASER "

The priority of the Pleaser is approval
from others.

I'm Right; You're Wrong

The purpose of this game is to avoid being proven wrong. The game can be played, regardless of the level of significance of the event or situation. Being declared right will achieve for the player dominance over the partner and control of the relationship. Both partners claim exclusive possession of the real facts. Each denies that the other partner has access to the facts. For example, one partner would say, "You were too drunk to know what kind of fool you were making of yourself." The possibility of equality is nonexistent in "I'm right; you're wrong." The players are more concerned with control than with the quality of the marriage relationship.

Accounting

In *Accounting*, the goal is to control events by a debit and credit system of bookkeeping. Each partner is interested in balancing his or her own account, rather than seeing that the marriage's joint account grows. For example, the husband says, "You decided on our vacation last year. Now it's my turn." The wife replies, "Yes, but you chose where we stayed, and we played tennis all the time instead of doing what I wanted." The husband answers, "However, we ate in the restaurants you chose." The wife responds, "Do you remember that we flew even though I wanted to drive and sightsee?"

Accounting is based on the assumption that life is a series of pluses and minuses with nothing in between. In playing the game, the partners are constantly on guard so that they are not taken advantage of. People who participate in psychological accounting feel inadequate. The game is a manifestation of a pessimistic life style that leaves little room for cooperation.

I DON'T WANT
TO TALK ABOUT IT!

Partners often play a silence game to avoid
losing an argument.

I Don't Want to Discuss It

Through silence a partner becomes invincible. As long as the partner remains silent, there is no chance for the other partner to claim a victory. This game permits only two responses—silence or "I don't want to talk about it." *I Don't Want to Discuss It* is easily initiated to avoid losing another game, just as a child fearing defeat might say, "I quit!"

This Is War

There is nothing subtle about *This Is War*. It is a full-fledged verbal battle. The cycle escalates, with each attack followed by retaliation with a verbal club. The underlying motive in the game is revenge. Partners who play *This Is War* act on the belief "I have been hurt by something you did or said. Now I'm hurting in return."

It's All Your Fault

This is the game-of-choice for injustice collectors, a blaming game. One partner says to the other, "It's all because of you." Since the advantage always lies with the attacker, it is important to strike first. The partner taking the initiative accuses the other of total responsibility for whatever is perceived as a mistake. The responding partner is immediately placed in a defensive position and, therefore, is more vulnerable.

What patterned reactions are you aware of in your marriage relationship? In other words, what games do you play? As you become aware of your patterned reactions, ask yourself, "What am I trying to hide? What am I hoping to win?"

Games destroy honest communication. A game is played to win. People pay a high price for victory in the games we have discussed. Gone is the opportunity to share openly. Lost is the caring atmosphere that exists in a game-free mature marriage.

Game-free Relationships

Marriage requires continuous dialogue to keep a couple in tune with each other. Through dialogue, partners share hopes, plans, and dreams. When communication is ineffective, the results may be misunderstanding, alienation, and loneliness—the enemies of marriage. By examining the way they communicate, partners can learn to avoid games. Regular encouragement meetings create the opportunity to develop understanding and to align goals.

The game-free relationship is characterized by flexibility and empathy. There is less emphasis on power, control, and winning. Game-free relationships produce less stress, and although winning is not emphasized, both partners feel like winners.

Here are alternative titles for the games discussed above that illustrate how we can replace competition with cooperation.

I'm Right; You're Wrong becomes *I can understand how you see it that way. You have a point.* Instead of attempting to prove "I'm right," a partner decides to examine the opposite point of view, and thus to show consideration for the other partner's beliefs and feelings. This does not mean surrender, but it does demonstrate understanding and acceptance.

Accounting becomes *Win/Win*, affirming that each partner has rights and responsibilities. Instead of focusing on personal gains and keeping score, there is an atmosphere of give-and-take without concern for who is ahead or behind.

I Don't Want to Discuss It becomes *This is Love. This is Love* removes the preoccupation with control and getting one's way. When conflict occurs, revenge and escalation are no longer acceptable alternatives. Instead, partners evaluate how their behavior will help them achieve or keep them from achieving the long-range goals for the relationship. Love becomes the uniting force in their relationship.

It's All Your Fault becomes *I'm Responsible.* By taking personal responsibility for their own behavior, the partners now move toward positive, mutually satisfying solutions to their conflicts.

To help you further in reaching a new understanding of your relationship, take time to play *The Relationship Game* described below. *The Relationship Game* is adapted from a therapeutic game developed by Theodore Rubin.[7] The basic goal of the game is for your marriage relationship to win. Therefore, during play your positive marriage goals take precedence over your individual goals. The game can't proceed if personal interest becomes more important than the relationship itself.

Play the game once a week for ten minutes. Each partner is the focus of attention during half of the session. The player beginning expresses a personal difficulty, stating the problem in a manner that demonstrates that he or she accepts responsibility for the problem. After the problem is expressed, the listening partner gives feedback to assure the partner who is sharing that what he or she has said has been understood. Then both partners focus on the problem, jointly seeking a solution. They explore together the belief, feeling, intention, and value that bring about this problem. What is shared should be considered confidential and should not be used later as a weapon.

If it is difficult to focus on a problem, begin by talking about your pride—your pride in being strong, right, morally superior, pleasing, and so on. Allow your mind to identify what is interfering with your relationship by using the process of free association.

As you play, try to avoid:

Blaming and fault-finding
Interrupting each other
Manipulating in order to get your way
Feeling abused and bitter, holding on to the victim position
Concern with being liked and desiring to please at all costs
Making a moral judgment
Expecting a reward or appreciation
Bullying of any kind whatsoever
Conscious lies, willful modifications, or exaggerations[8]

The goal is to help you perceive and understand without judging each other. As you participate regularly in this game, your marriage relationship will benefit from more open communication, mutual respect, and empathy. You can begin to replace pessimistic assumptions about marriage relationships with positive feelings based on your own experiences.

The Relationship Game will help you become aware of behaviors you can choose daily to create a loving relationship. When we are learning to play a game we have to focus consciously on the rules of the game in order to learn to play correctly. It is only later that the rules become so familiar that we play without needing to give a great deal of thought to the game.

Similarly, while we are learning to create a more loving relationship, we focus our efforts on developing new ways of relating. At the same time we "unlearn" less effective habits of relating. The following guidelines can help you focus on behaviors that help create a loving relationship.

1. Know and accept yourself.
2. Remember that we each create our own happiness. Neither our partner nor our marriage can *make* us happy. Stop blaming, demanding, and accusing.
3. Share your life with your partner whenever possible, but feel secure when you are not with your partner.
4. Share your deepest feelings with your partner.
5. "Ask for what you want. Enjoy what you get."[9]
6. Appreciate your partner and help your partner to feel loveable.
7. Enjoy the unity in your relationship.

References

1. Sidney B. Simon, Leland W. Howe, and Howard Kirschenbaum, *Values Clarification* (NY: A & W Publishers, 1978), pp. 30-34. Excerpts reprinted with permission of A & W Publishers.
2. Karen Horney's description of personality themes is discussed in Theodore I. Rubin, *One to One: Understanding Personal Relationships*, (NY: Viking Press, 1983), p. 14.
3. Harold Mosak, *On Purpose*, (Chicago: Alfred Adler Institute, 1977) and Bernard H. Shulman, *Contributions to Individual Psychology*, (Chicago: Alfred Adler Institute, 1973).
4. Don Dinkmeyer, W. L. Pew, and Don Dinkmeyer, Jr., *Adlerian Counseling and Psychotherapy*, (Monterey, CA: Brooks/Cole, 1979).
5. Eric Berne, *Games People Play*, (NY: Grove Press, 1964).
6. Gerald Mozdzierz and Thomas Lottman, "Games Married Couples Play: Adlerian View," *Journal of Individual Psychology*, 29 (November 1973): 182-194.

7. Theodore I. Rubin, *One to One: Understanding Personal Relationships,* (NY: Viking Press, 1983).

8. Ibid, 233-234.

9. Ken Keyes, Jr., *A Conscious Person's Guide to Relationships,* (St. Mary, KY: Living Love Publications, 1979), p. 58.

Questions

1. What factors form our life style?

2. How can we identify our true values?

3. Do any of the life style types mentioned in this chapter exist in your marriage?

4. What are some ways that your original family atmosphere affects your marriage?

5. Describe the four priorities of life style. Do you feel you are maintaining one of these priorities at this time?

6. Which of the marital games have you experienced?

7. How can you build a game-free relationship?

8. What did you learn by playing *The Relationship Game*?

Activity for the Week

Continue Daily Dialogue and hold an Encouragement Meeting three times this week.

Do the Values Clarification exercise, following the directions in Chapter 3.

To help you assess your goals and progress, fill in *My Plan*.

In writing, answer the following questions: *What are the goals in your relationship? What do you want to start doing in your relationship? What do you want to stop doing in your relationship?*

Listen to "Relationship Development for Couples" on *Time to Relax and Imagine*, your personal audiocassette.*

---

*The cassette, *Time to Relax and Imagine*, is available from American Guidance Service, Circle Pines, MN. An order form is provided in the back of this book.

1. In a marriage, partners have a system of relating to each other. Your marriage system reflects your goals, beliefs, and priorities as individuals and as a couple.

2. Your life style reflects your beliefs, values, intentions, perceptions, and priorities.

3. The life style we bring to our marriage relationship is often a reflection of the family atmosphere in which we were raised.

4. Four priorities of life style are control, superiority, pleasing, and comfort seeking.

5. Games are sophisticated, patterned manuevers that are destructive to a marriage relationship. Games focus on individual power rather than on the growth of the relationship.

6. As you become aware of games in your marriage, you can choose to replace them with more honest, open ways of communicating.

7. Game-free relationships are characterized by flexibility and empathy.

8. *The Relationship Game* is a method to help your relationship take precedence over individual goals.

MY ◆ PLAN

Ways I can encourage _____

_____

Strengths I can use to improve the relationship _____

_____

Ways I can show I care or appreciate _____

_____

Ways I can improve my communication _____

_____

Effective ways I can resolve conflict _____

_____

I am ready and willing to change my behavior in the following way(s): _____

_____

MY PROGRESS IN APPLYING THESE SKILLS	I am doing this more	I need to do this more	I remain about the same
Listening to feelings			
Communicating honestly			
Encouraging			
Daily dialogue			
Communicating love			
Encouragement meetings			
Marriage meetings			
Resolving conflict effectively			
Demonstrating specific caring behavior			
Choosing a better marriage			
Spending time with my partner			

Partners often have difficulty expressing what they really feel.

Honesty and Openness: Being Congruent

Communication is to a relationship what breathing is to maintaining life.

Virginia Satir[1]

To be congruent is to express what we are feeling and experiencing at the moment. In a congruent relationship a couple can be who they really are and say what they really think and feel. When couples openly and honestly express thoughts and feelings, true intimacy grows and grievances can be revealed and resolved.

In many marriages partners find it difficult to express their true feelings and thoughts. What do they fear will happen to their marriage? Why do they find it necessary to hide their feelings? To reveal one's self is to risk rejection. To reveal one's feelings opens the door to being misunderstood. To be rejected and misunderstood by our marriage partner can be a painful, even devastating experience. Unfortunately, our fears and self-doubts separate us from the honesty and openness we need in order to make our marriage healthy.

When we understand the price we pay by holding on to our fears and self-doubts, we can begin to release our fears and create an atmosphere that will allow open expression of thoughts and feelings. A relationship built on honest and open communication is a congruent relationship.

This chapter will help you identify ways you can begin to communicate in an open, honest manner. To be congruent you may need to develop some new skills and new understanding. The main points to be covered are as follows:

1. We practice congruency by expressing what we are feeling and experiencing at the moment and encouraging our partner's feedback on what is heard and experienced.

2. To be congruent requires courage, especially sufficient courage to risk rejection.

3. In a congruent relationship the partners individually practice self-acceptance, accept responsibility for thoughts and feelings, cooperate willingly, and communicate clearly.

4. Your present style of communication can be adapted to allow you to create a more congruent relationship.

Expressing Thoughts and Feelings

We practice congruency by expressing what we are feeling and experiencing at the moment. If we feel hurt or angry, we trust our partner enough to honestly reveal what we are feeling, without attacking. In a marriage, congruent communication allows each partner to know what the other is feeling, without guessing. Congruent communication gives the partners opportunities to be empathic. When there is lack of congruence people have a tendency to "gunny-sack" feelings. They collect grievances in a mental gunny-sack and extract them later when it is to their advantage. Often what is gunny-sacked is used later as a weapon. Since partners are often unaware of the negative feelings they have been collecting, there is little opportunity to change behavior or improve the relationship. When we share our thoughts and feelings, we show that we trust our partner enough to reveal who we really are. Congruent communication eliminates gunny-sacking and allows us to share without the need to get even for past hurts. Our sharing does not turn into a session in which we demand that the other change. Sharing gives us the opportunity to give feedback.

One method of sabotaging a marital relationship is the practice of using words that convey the opposite of what we are really feeling. For example, you may say to your partner, "It's okay if you go without me," when it isn't okay, or "I'm glad you got the promotion," when actually you feel hurt, sad, or jealous.

The Role of Courage in Becoming Congruent

It takes courage to express feelings even though we are concerned that we might be misunderstood. If partners care enough about their relationship, they will be courageous in sharing perceptions and feelings. No issues will be off limits. They will talk about their differences, feelings of anger, rejection, or despair.

To be courageous requires that you not only express emotions but also take responsibility for the emotions. To be congruent in your communication, share your feelings in a way that demonstrates you own the feeling, rather than that you believe the feeling was caused by your partner. For example, you can say "I feel you are pressuring me to do this your way," rather than "Get off my back."

A technique to use in expressing feelings is to state your feelings in "I messages." An "I message" has three parts.

1. Describe the behavior without blaming.
2. State your feelings.
3. State what the consequences might be.

Here is an example of an "I message:" "When you are late coming home at night, I feel anxious because I think you may have been in an accident."

In the above example, "When you are late coming home at night . . ." describes the behavior; ". . . I feel anxious . . ." states your feeling; and ". . . because I think you may have been in an accident," states the consequences you fear.

How could the following statements be expressed as "I messages?"

"You make me so angry when you interrupt me!"

1. Describe the behavior:_____

_____

2. State the feeling:_____

_____

3. State what the consequences might be:_____

_____

"It's your fault that I'm in a bad mood. You forgot our anniversary again."

1. Describe the behavior:_____

_____

2. State the feeling:_____

_____

3. State what the consequences might be:_____

_____

The next time you hear yourself expressing a feeling by saying "It's your fault . . ." or "You make me . . ." think of how you could have expressed the feeling with an "I message."

By acccepting responsibility for feelings, partners can change a relationship from one of complaining to one of open, honest communication.

Taking Risks

In addition to demonstrating courage by accepting responsibility for our feelings, being congruent requires us to have the courage to take risks. Risking means doing something we haven't done before or trying it a new way.

Many partners play roles in the hope that they will be liked for what they pretend to be rather than for who they are. Self-disclosure requires courage. It is easier to play the game of looking good than to honestly reveal our feelings. By learning to risk being rejected, even long-estab-

CAROL LOVES TO ENTERTAIN!

I'M THE CHEF

Many partners play roles in the hope that they will be liked for what they pretend to be rather than for who they are.

lished patterns can be changed to each person's benefit.

Coretta always got up early on Sunday morning to prepare dinner before going to church. When she returned from church, she served dinner and did the dishes. It was mid-afternoon before she was free of chores. One week Coretta said, "I dread Sundays because I feel trapped by the cooking routine. Why don't we join our friends who go out for brunch every Sunday?" By risking, Coretta was able to communicate her feelings and find a satisfactory alternative to a long-established pattern.

Risks are necessary if we are unwilling to settle for a superficial, dishonest relationship. A couple who risks being emotionally honest is courageous and caring. Each partner wants to enjoy the benefits of openly communicating beliefs, values, feelings, and intentions. Congruence gives couples greater understanding and empathy for each other. Honest communication is the only avenue to genuine togetherness.

Stan is bothered by Diane's pattern of constantly nagging and scolding the children about the care of their rooms. He feels the nagging is making them "parent deaf" and resistant. He dislikes the way the children ignore their mother. When he talks to Diane about the situation, she feels he is interfering. Stan has tried to remain silent, but he realizes he is very angry and the anger is interfering with his relationship with Diane. Stan decides to take a risk.

Stan: "Diane, I'd like to share some feelings. Are you ready to hear them?"

Diane: "Not if you're going to attack me!"

Stan: "I'd like to share how I feel so we can come to a better understanding of each other. When I don't share my feelings, I find myself getting angry at you and the anger interferes with our relationship."

Diane: "Well, okay, but I'm not sure how I'll react."

Stan: "I feel very tense and angry when you nag the children about their rooms. I think it's ineffective to nag and you are losing an opportunity to influence them in a positive manner."

Diane: "I just can't stand the mess they leave."

Stan: "You're upset about the mess, and I understand that. But I don't think nagging is accomplishing what you want."

Diane: "It's *easy* to criticize. Do you have any suggestions?"

Stan: "I'm not sure what will work, but I have some ideas. Maybe the four of us could meet to discuss what is expected and get the children's ideas about what can be done."

Diane: "How will talking with them help when I talk to them about it every day?"

Stan: "Maybe I can take a more active role and say what is expected. We can also learn what is important to them."

Diane: "I doubt this will work, but I must admit what I'm doing isn't working. I don't like being criticized, but I am glad you shared how you feel."

Diane and Stan's relationship will grow as they continue to take responsibility for sharing feelings instead of gunny-sacking and harboring resentments. This open, congruent sharing will produce greater trust, mutual respect, and cooperation.

A partner who fears rejection may actually encourage rejection by a closed and challenging attitude. For example, a grin-and-bear-it facial expression may reflect an individual's unwillingness to either hear or express feelings. Rather than expressing anger or hurt the partner hides these feelings. Such behavior is self-defeating.

Feedback is an important part of the process of sharing feelings. When we express our own feelings we encourage our partner to share feelings and ideas. By our feedback we indicate to our partner, "This is the way I am experiencing you." Feedback communicates feelings with no demand for change, but change often results from honest, open communication.

If the fear of rejection prevents partners from sharing, they give up the most precious gift they could ever possess—a genuinely intimate relationship.

Self-acceptance

The individual who is self-accepting is more likely to want to establish a congruent relationship. Lacking self-acceptance, an individual may be working toward the goals of attention, power, revenge, and excusing shortcomings—goals that are counter to the goal of cooperation. The courage to take risks to develop a congruent relationship is therefore an outgrowth of self-acceptance. Self-accepting individuals recognize their strengths and know how to use these strengths to improve the marriage relationship. When we are self-accepting we are more likely to encourage and accept feedback, and to be concerned about the needs and welfare of our partner. We avoid the "me first" tyrant-oriented marriage with one or both partners who think mainly of self or the "me last" victim or martyr marriage.

The combination of self-acceptance and willingness to cooperate for the common good creates an atmosphere in which congruent communication is possible.

Partners may display inadequacy in order to excuse themselves from meeting others' expectations.

Styles of Communication

Even though partners believe they are self-accepting and interested in cooperation, their styles of communication may limit their ability to establish a congruent relationship. The way you communicate in your marriage reflects to some degree the style of communication you learned as you were growing up. Your style of communicating was the way you survived in the human relationships you encountered at home and in school. As an adult you may be continuing the style of communication even though it is no longer in line with your beliefs and goals, and in fact may be separating you from the cooperation and understanding you desire.

Virginia Satir describes four communication styles that have a negative influence on our relationships. Individuals who use these styles are called *Placaters, Blamers, Super Reasonable* communicators, or *Irrelevant* communicators.

Placaters believe they are always wrong, and others are always right. In order to be loved, Placaters strive to please and keep everyone happy. In marital quarrels, Placaters give in. The partner of a Placater tends to feel annoyed since there is no challenge.

Blamers attack others, indicating that other people never do anything right. Blamers believe they must demand cooperation in order to get it. Blamers are always right and are controlling. The partner of a Blamer constantly feels criticized and challenged.

When a Blamer is paired with a Placater, the styles appear to be in harmony.

Super Reasonable communicators focus on being intellectually superior to others and constantly let people know they are intelligent. They ignore feelings since logic and ideas are all that count. Lack of empathy and understanding in the relationship causes the partner of the Super Reasonable communicator to feel a lack of connection and belonging.

Irrelevant communicators focus on obtaining attention at all costs. They do not consider anyone's needs but their own. The partner of the Irrelevant communicator feels insignificant.[2]

These four styles of communication are manipulative and controlling. The Placater leads people to feel guilty or to respond with pity. The Blamer stimulates fear and feelings of inadequacy. The Super Reasonable communicator creates distance by a barrage of words devoid of feeling, causing others to feel inferior or inept. The Irrelevant communicator gains power by distracting and disrupting.

A person may use any or all of these styles of communication. The style chosen is based on the individual's perception of the demands of the situation. We use communication to achieve a purpose. However, unless we become consciously aware of what we are trying to achieve by our communication, we may continue using a style that once seemed effective but no longer helps us achieve our goals. Ineffective communication interferes with closeness and cooperation and prevents us from disclosing ourselves honestly.

Do you recognize your style of communicating in the above descriptions? What style do you most frequently use? What are situations in which you placate, striving to please at all costs? When do you become a blamer, demanding your way? When do you communicate from a super reasonable point of view, ignoring feelings? When is your communication primarily irrelevant, focusing mainly on your own needs?

Let's look at how one couple communicates ineffectively:

Jerry: "I'm in a hurry. Where did you put the car keys?"

Clara: "I haven't driven your car, nor do I know where your keys are. You're always misplacing things."

Jerry: "Don't blame me. You're responsible for the house. I always put the keys on the desk and they aren't there. You must have moved them."

Clara: "I'm not the only one responsible for this house, and I'm certainly not responsible for your keys. You're the one who leaves stuff lying around. If you weren't so messy you could find something now and then."

Jerry and Clara are obviously two Blamers. Now let's see how the conversation would proceed if Jerry were married to someone with a different style of communication.

Jerry: "I'm in a hurry. Where did you put the car keys?"

Sheila: "I'm sorry. I guess they must have been misplaced. Don't worry, I'll find them."

Jerry: "You are always making me late."

Sheila: "I know. I just don't keep as organized as I should. But I'll do better."

Jerry: "If you really want to help me, keep track of my things."

When a Blamer is paired with a Placater, the styles appear to be in harmony. The Blamer has a willing listener and the Placater has someone to attempt to please. However, each partner's potential to grow may be reduced.

If you are using one of these forms of communication, remember that it was the way you survived in the past. Accept where you are now! Be encouraged that you have discovered your communication style. If you are uncomfortable with the style and want to change it, your intention is in itself a sign of progress. You have the power to choose a more congruent style of communication.

Patterns of Communication

When we communicate, there is high probability that the message we intended to convey will not be received exactly as we wish. It is common to say to someone, "That is what I said, but that's not really what I meant." When we talk to each other, the person listening automatically processes the message in terms of his or her own beliefs, values, goals, and experience. Because we bring our own perceptions to any situation, misunderstandings frequently occur. When we say, "That's how I see it," and our partner says, "I don't see why you can't

understand," we are in a situation resulting from two different points of view.

Different points of view are to be expected and are not, by themselves, harmful to a marriage relationship if the beliefs of the couple are in harmony. However, if communication consistently produces misunderstanding, hurt, or anger, one or both partners may be operating from mistaken self-defeating beliefs. Your beliefs help determine your feelings, i.e. your spontaneous emotional response to a situation.

In your marriage, communication difficulties frequently can be resolved by becoming aware of the way you commonly react to each other. The way your partner usually reacts can tell you a great deal about the goal you are trying to reach by your communication. That goal, in turn, is a reflection of your belief.

How does your partner typically feel as a result of something you have said that has caused disagreement? Is your partner annoyed, angry, hurt, or deeply discouraged? By noticing your partner's reaction you can become aware of the

By noticing your partner's reaction, you can become aware of your goal. If the response is annoyance, the goal must be attention.

goal of your communication, even though you may not have known you had a goal. If your partner feels annoyed, you may have been seeking attention. If your partner feels angry, you may have intended to achieve power or control. If your partner feels hurt, you may have been trying to get even. Your partner's feeling of resignation and discouragement suggests that you were displaying inadequacy in order to excuse yourself from meeting expectations.

Matt and Maria are having a conflict about where to spend Thanksgiving vacation. Matt wants to stay home and Maria wants them to visit her parents. Matt says, "Let's be rational about this. The roads are always icy in November. It doesn't make sense to drive anywhere." He gets no response, so he becomes more demanding. His feelings energize his opinion and he states, "I'm calling your folks to tell them we can't make it this year. You'll be glad I did." Maria feels hurt and decides to get even. She says, "Well, if you're calling them, tell them I'll be flying in on Wednesday night!"

Matt used his feelings to try to achieve his goal of power. Maria's feelings were directed toward her goal of revenge. Matt appears to be operating from the belief, "I must be in control." Matt's goal or purpose is to be in control. Maria's belief may be, "I have treated you right. It is unfair of you to treat me this way." Her belief allows her to give herself permission to find a way to get even. The chart below summarizes the interaction of our beliefs and purposes, and emotional transactions that usually result.

Chart 4A

How Beliefs and Purposes Affect Behavior			
Belief	Purpose	Emotion Experienced by Partner	Transaction
I must be in control.	To control	Anger	Battling or giving in
I have treated you right. It is unfair of you to treat me this way.	To give self permission	Hurt, revenge	Finding ways to get even
I must please to have a place	To be accepted	Feel pleased but despair at demands for approval	Serving and being served
I am inadequate	To reduce all expectations	Giving up, confusion	Manipulating into being excused

Chart 4A illustrates how your beliefs are parallel to your purposes. When a belief or purpose is activated, it leads to a predictable emotional transaction.

When you understand your goal or purpose, you can decide whether this goal is worth the bad feelings and poor relationship it produces. To improve your relationship you need to give up mistaken perceptions and goals.

We often feel we have power if we have control or are getting our own way. A more effective feeling of power comes from being responsible for our own behavior or, in other words, from being more independent. When we decide to be responsible for our own behavior, we experience a tremendous feeling of power and self-satisfaction. When we are responsible for our behavior and feelings, we no longer believe that someone made us do something or feel a certain way. We control and own our actions and emotions. We can state, "I was late because I did not start on time," or "I am angry because I allowed myself to get upset." This contrasts with saying, "You made me late," or "You make me mad."

When you become aware of your real power, you become more interested in cooperating, in being fair, and in treating your partner with respect. You no longer feel overwhelmed by hurt or revenge. You don't have to win. You are more willing to practice give-and-take in your marriage, and your marriage is characterized by encouragement.

What Message Are You Really Communicating?

The message we intend to send is not always the one that is received. Nonverbal cues such as tone of voice and facial expression influence what we hear. Also, what we think the other person really intends colors the message we receive. If our partner says "I accept the fact that you must put in long hours at work," but the words sound resentful, the resentment is the message we are more likely to attend to. Even if the words truly indicate our partner's feeling, the message did not seem to be congruent. The resentment in our partner's voice suggests that what was being said and what was being felt were not in harmony. The message was not believable.

Developing Your Ability to be Congruent

To develop a more congruent relationship, it is helpful to become aware of how you typically respond to situations in your marriage. Rather than respond out of habit, you can learn to choose a response that allows you to express your feelings in a way that is beneficial to your relationship. John Gottman recommends an editing technique.[3] The process of editing your communication is similar to the process of editing a written document. Editing retains the message but assures that it is presented as clearly as possible with the potential reader in mind. The purpose of editing responses in your marriage is to allow you to express your thoughts openly and honestly without being insensitive to your partner's needs. Editing contributes to your relationship because you develop the ability to be as polite to your partner as you are to strangers. By editing, you can be sure your response promotes cooperation rather than competition.

Here is a situation that might occur without editing. When you get home from work your partner asks, "Would you be willing to fix supper tonight? I know it's my night to cook, but I'm just exhausted." You respond, "Hey, I'm exhausted too. You just couldn't have had as grueling a day as I did. Don't rush supper, though. I'll take a little nap and give you an extra half hour."

With editing, you might have responded, "It must have been that kind of day for both of us. I'm wiped out too. Why don't we rest a few minutes and then I'll go pick up some hamburgers?" This response would allow you to be open and honest, and at the same time sensitive to your partner.

To edit a response you need to be aware of the possibility of delaying your response so that you can choose to be congruent and at the same time choose a response that does not separate you from each other.

Encouragement meetings also help you become more congruent. By regularly taking time for encouragement meetings that focus on what is positive, you are more likely to respond in encouraging ways at other times. The sense of belonging becomes a central focus that you will want to protect.

Guidelines for Being Congruent

1. Be courageous. Take risks in things that matter.
2. Be self-accepting. Value yourself and have the courage to be imperfect.
3. Communicate clearly. Seek feedback to clarify how you are being heard.
4. Communicate your thoughts and feelings openly.
5. Accept change as a way of life and learn to welcome it.
6. Have a positive purpose. Be involved in what you do and find personal meaning in what you do.
7. Focus on the potential and resources in your relationship instead of the limitations.
8. When sharing your feelings, be empathic and sensitive to how your partner feels.

References

1. Virginia Satir, *Making Contact*, (Millbrae, CA: Celestial Arts, 1976).
2. Ibid.
3. John Gottman, *A Couple's Guide to Communication*, (Champaign, IL: Research Press, 1976).

Questions

1. What is the value of being congruent? What are the risks?
2. If a person "gunny-sacks" feelings, what problems may result?
3. What is an "I message?" What are the benefits of using "I messages?"
4. Think of risks you have taken in your marriage. How did this risk-taking affect your relationship?
5. Why does feedback create greater intimacy in a relationship?
6. Virginia Satir identified four styles of communication that may harm a relationship. What is the first step in changing a harmful style of communication?
7. How does your style of communication affect your marriage?
8. What is the editing technique? How can editing help you be more congruent?

Activity for the Week

Continue Daily Dialogue and Encouragement Meetings.

Practice congruent communication with your partner. Share what you are feeling openly. Let your partner know whether he or she heard accurately. When your partner shares, listen empathetically.

1. We are congruent when we express what we are feeling and experiencing at the moment.

2. To be congruent requires courage.

3. In a marriage congruent communication allows each partner to know what the other is feeling without guessing.

4. "I messages" help us express our thoughts and feelings without placing blame on our partner. When we use an "I message" we say, "When you _____, I feel _____ because I _____."

5. To be congruent we must develop the courage to take risks.

6. Self-acceptance is the basis for a congruent relationship.

7. Four communication styles that negatively influence our relationship are: the Placater, the Blamer, the Super Reasonable communicator, and the Irrelevant communicator.

8. You can learn to express your feelings and thoughts openly without being insensitive to your partner's needs.

MY ◆ PLAN

Ways I can encourage _____

_____

Strengths I can use to improve the relationship _____

_____

Ways I can show I care or appreciate _____

_____

Ways I can improve my communication _____

_____

Effective ways I can resolve conflict _____

_____

I am ready and willing to change my behavior in the following way(s): _____

_____

MY PROGRESS IN APPLYING THESE SKILLS	I am doing this more	I need to do this more	I remain about the same
Listening to feelings			
Communicating honestly			
Encouraging			
Daily dialogue			
Communicating love			
Encouragement meetings			
Marriage meetings			
Resolving conflict effectively			
Demonstrating specific caring behavior			
Choosing a better marriage			
Spending time with my partner			

Communication is one of the most powerful factors
influencing the quality of a relationship.

Communication: Basis for an Effective Relationship

Couples often share the same house and bed but feel they are strangers. They want to share and be intimate, but they find themselves growing apart. They communicate ideas and facts but rarely share their personal feelings about each other. The search for intimacy and honest caring is one of the major challenges of life. Intimacy begins when partners really listen to each other and share feelings, even though by sharing feelings they risk rejection. When they share feelings and give feedback without expecting or demanding change, partners demonstrate that they care about each other and their relationship more than they care about maintaining peace at any price. When a couple creates a climate in which they can share feelings, they find the intimacy that frees them to be themselves and, in turn, nourishes their marriage.

Communication is one of the most powerful factors influencing the quality of a relationship. When effective communication is developed in a marriage, a couple is able to solve problems and sharing, empathy, and understanding increase. And, therefore, intimacy increases as well. It is through communication that the relationship either grows or is destroyed.

How intimate and meaningful is your communication?

How do you and your partner avoid intimacy?

How do you and your partner create intimacy?

Factors that Influence Communication

The way you communicate in your marriage is greatly influenced by your family background. In early childhood, you figured out what you had to do to get what you wanted, often by trial and error. The communication that worked for you as a child was basically compatible with your family's style of communication. As you matured and gained insight, you added your own rules or beliefs to help you cope with life. The communication patterns you developed earlier may continue to affect your life, however. To gain insight into communication patterns that influenced you as a child and may continue to influence you now, answer the following questions:

Was your family cooperative and trusting, or competitive and challenging? What kind of communication did you observe between your father and mother? Were they passively cooperative? Was one dominant and the other a peacemaker? Do you work to avoid or to continue your parents' pattern of communication in your marriage?

What you consciously or unconsciously choose to model from your family background influences your marriage communication. If your family expressed negative feelings frequently and loudly, you may assume that is the way to talk things out, and you may resent your partner's unwillingness to argue. In turn, your partner's attitude about expressing feelings may have been influenced by family patterns.

In addition to the psychological atmosphere in which you were raised, your birth order position also influences your marriage relationship and communication. The oldest child in a family is accustomed to being first and dominant. Because oldest children are accustomed to telling others what to do and in getting their way, oldest children may find it difficult to compromise. When two oldest children marry, they may both struggle to be in charge and control decisions. Second children tend to be rebellious. If both partners are second children, they may continually rebel against each other. Youngest children are often used to having things done for them. If two youngest children marry, each may expect the other to carry out major responsibilities.

Middle children have often learned to compromise and be aware of the needs of others. A marriage of two middle children may reap the benefits of give-and-take.

An oldest child married to a youngest child is often initially a compatible relationship. One may be accustomed to controlling, and the other expects to have decisions made. Eventually the relationship may become a power struggle.

An only child may be either very dependent or extremely responsible.

Although birth order alone does not determine our perception of human relationships, birth order does have an influence. However, the way an individual interprets his or her role in the family has an even greater influence than the actual birth order position.

How Assumptions and Beliefs Influence Communication

Our beliefs influence communication with our partner. Positive beliefs about ourselves and about life lead to communication that brings happiness and satisfaction to a marriage. If we were raised in an encouraging home, or if we are fortunate to have an atmosphere of encouragement in our present life, we may have positive beliefs. The most important permanent source of positive beliefs, however, is our ability to affirm ourselves.

Unfortunately, we may be operating from negative beliefs or assumptions that discourage or promote competition rather than cooperation. If you believe you must be right, every conflict is unresolved until your partner surrenders. If you believe you cannot survive rejection, you will strive to please your partner at all costs. If you believe you must be in control in order to be recognized, you can expect conflict to be a part of your relationship. If you believe you must be perfect, you can

expect disappointment because all humans are imperfect.

Negative beliefs can be a major source of irritation, bringing discord to a relationship. Our beliefs influence our feelings, actions, and communication. Through practicing self-affirmation and through encouraging each other regularly we can replace negative beliefs with positive beliefs, such as:

I want to cooperate.

I feel good about myself.

I feel equal to others.

People treat me fairly.

Feelings Energize Communication

Feelings give energy to our communication. The strength of a feeling is a clear indication of how important an issue is to us. Or, to express it in another way, the intensity of the feeling tells us how strongly we hold a certain belief and how strongly we want to achieve a certain goal. Feelings are not by themselves good or bad, but they can be used in a positive or negative way. They are reliable sources of information and can be used as tools in strengthening our relationship.

In communicating with our partner, we need to listen not only to what is being said (the message),

Not expressing feelings blocks a relationship.

but also the feeling. Missing or failing to recognize the feeling in a message can mean that the entire message may be misunderstood. We might conclude, for example, that our partner is mildly disturbed or annoyed when in fact the feeling is anger or deep hurt. Until we understand the underlying feeling, we cannot effectively understand the message. Feelings are the seasoning in a message. They help us get the flavor so that we can go beyond the content of the message and understand the beliefs and intentions. Awareness of feelings prevents relationships from becoming dull. Boredom and lack of involvement in some relationships is due to the failure to share feelings openly. By communicating your feelings to your partner and by listening for the feeling in your partner's communication, you allow growth in your relationship.

To become responsible for your feelings, become aware of what you are feeling. When you recognize the feeling, own it by saying, "I am feeling . . ." As you recognize and own the feeling, and risk sharing the feeling, you become aware of how your perception has been influenced by your feeling. When you understand your feeling, you can choose what to do about the situation. Often when a feeling is identified we find that our perception of a situation changes.

Understanding Goals and Intentions

The entire message in our communication includes feelings, beliefs, and goals or intentions. Through listening and providing feedback, we assure our partner that we understand what is being communicated. Demonstrating that we understand what our partner is feeling is vital, but we can go farther in our demonstration of understanding by identifying each other's goals. A deeply satisfying relationship is possible when we understand each other's goals and help each other work toward achieving goals.

Listen to the entire message including the feeling, belief, and goals. Give feedback that indicates your understanding. Here are two examples:

Message	Response
"I talked with Helen about her negative attitude toward her brother, but she got angry and stormed off. I'm confused and don't know what to do."	"When Helen became angry you felt discouraged. You're not sure what to do next."
"You expect me to work, keep house, and manage the kids while you're off traveling, playing golf, or making business contacts. If you don't pitch in and help me, I'm quitting my job."	"You feel I expect too much of you, and you are going to quit your job if I don't help you.

In the situations described above the person responding considered the beliefs, feelings and intentions. How would you respond to the following messages?

Message	Your Response
"Can't you ever miss an evening meeting? I'm here alone every night!"	_____
"I'd like to go out with the couple next door, but you're always tired. I feel we have no social life."	_____
"I've worked ten years for the company and now they let me go with two-weeks' notice. I'm disgusted!"	_____
"I feel like I can't keep regular contact with my friends without you getting angry."	_____

Roadblocks to Couple Communication

Our attitudes and beliefs can prevent our marriage relationship from improving. The following attitudes block communication and cause conflict or interfere with problem solving:

1. *"I'm right."*—I don't need to hear what you have to say. I'm just that way. You know how I am.

2. *"It's your problem."*—Don't expect me to bail you out. Take care of it yourself. They are your relatives. If you had only listened to me in the first place, this wouldn't have happened.

3. *"You should anticipate my desires and feelings."*—By now you should know me. Why do we have to discuss it; can't you guess what I'm feeling?

4. *"If we really love each other, why do we have to talk about this?"*—Love should conquer all.

If you have one of these attitudes, recognize how you may be setting up a roadblock preventing your own happiness. Choose a new attitude.

Vertical and Horizontal Communication

Hugh Allred and Thomas Graff have developed a systematic approach for improving communication between partners.[1] They describe communication as either level or vertical. When we practice level communication we seek to understand, negotiate, encourage, and reveal feelings. When we practice vertical communication, we draw attention to self, boss others, maintain or create distance, and/or surrender.[2]

Soliciting Attention

Attention seekers expend great effort getting others involved with them. They may interrupt, monopolize, boast, charm, ask for special attention, showcase their accomplishments, and keep others waiting. Their relationships tend to be superficial, resulting in resentment and distance. Personal growth is limited.

Bossing or Punishing

These people tend to lecture, give orders, talk down, probe, show hostility or anger, find fault, blame, and ridicule. Anger and resentment result from this type of communication. There is continuous conflict.

Creating or Maintaining Distance

Impersonal, mechanical communication increases the distance between people and creates superficial relationships. People who are aloof, superficial, evasive, and unwilling to become genuinely involved create or maintain distance. Sometimes they use humor to avoid contact. Their partners often reach out to others to find warmth, acceptance, genuineness, and friendship.

Having different priorities can create distance.

Surrendering

A pattern of giving up or deferring to others often occurs when one partner is bossy or punishing. People who surrender, or give in, fail to assert themselves and eventually lose their self-esteem. They may, however, collect grievances and try to get even with the partner later on.

Unhappy relationships commonly are based on the mistaken belief that to be important we must be superior to others. Allred and Graff point out that the goals in vertical communication are position, prestige, and power. The focus in the marriage may be on being more than your partner—more competent, more right, more noble. In a strongly aggressive relationship, either partner may become discouraged and give up.

Persons who relate vertically tend to be negative, critical, and destructive of the relationship. By focusing on mistakes and errors they overlook the positive. Persons who relate vertically may keep their partners busy working for them and, in the process, the partners are prevented from developing their own talents and thus competing for the spotlight.

Relationships can be improved if we identify and eliminate destructive communication patterns associated with vertical communication and increase the constructive patterns of level communication.

Relationships can be improved if we eliminate destructive communication patterns such as talking down to our partner.

Improving Couple Communication

Great progress can be made when both partners are willing to work on their communication. If one partner is resistant, the task is more difficult. However, since you are responsible only for your own behavior, it is not your job to change your partner. As you change, you influence your partner. If you are more empathic and understanding, your partner may choose to communicate with greater understanding also.

Level communication allows you to be open, flexible, honest, and genuine. When you communicate on a level, equal plane, you demonstrate that you accept responsibility for your behavior and are sensitive to your partner's feelings. A level communicator observes and shares opinions, understands, negotiates and commits, encourages, and discloses feelings openly.[3]

Sharing Opinions

Rather than centering on who is right and who is wrong, partners who practice level communication consider each other's ideas and express their own ideas without fear of rejection.

The following examples illustrate level ways of sharing opinions:

"I felt uncomfortable when you were late, and I'm really happy you are here."

"I felt angry that you invited them when I'm so busy."

Seeking to Understand

By asking each other questions, and by giving feedback, a couple can clarify for each other what is said or felt. When we seek to understand our partner's feelings and thoughts, we demonstrate caring and appreciation.

Examples:

"Tell me how you feel when I don't go to parties at your office."

"I get the impression you're fearful about the new job you've been offered, but you intend to accept it."

"I feel you believe that sex between us is primarily for your pleasure and that my needs are unimportant."

In the process of negotiation, explore alternatives until you reach a satisfactory agreement.

Negotiating and Committing

In the process of negotiation, various alternatives are explored that lead to a new agreement. Negotiation is done in an atmosphere in which each person is treated as an equal. All ideas are considered with mutual respect.

Example:

Sakan: "I have more than I can do with my job, taking the kids to soccer practice or games almost every night, and painting the house. I get discouraged because there is no way to do it all."

Michiko: "You're feeling overwhelmed."

Sakan: "I feel that my needs don't carry any weight around here."

Michiko: "I was not aware how badly you feel. I'll see if we can work out a car pool for soccer on the nights I work. Should we hire someone to help you with the painting?"

Encouraging

Encouragement communicates understanding, support, and empathy. When we recognize effort by encouraging, our partner's self-esteem grows.

Examples:

"I like your attitude."

"I'm sure you can do it."

"You're doing much better."

"Together we can handle this."

> ### Guidelines for Improving Your Communication
> 1. Be aware of the feelings being shared.
> 2. Be aware of the intentions being shared.
> 3. Be aware of the beliefs being shared.
> 4. Strive for level, equal communication.
> 5. Be empathic. Hear, identify, and verbalize the other person's feelings.
> 6. Be responsible for your feelings.
> 7. Free each other to be. Encourage uniqueness.

References

1. G. Hugh Allred and Thomas T. Graff, *Couples' Handbook for Effective Communication*, (Provo, UT: Brigham Young University Press, 1979).
2. G. Hugh Allred, *How to Strengthen Your Marriage and Family*, (Provo, UT: Brigham Young University Press, 1976).
3. Allred and Graff, 1979.

Questions

1. How can partners create a more intimate relationship?
2. What factors influence the way you and your partner communicate?
3. How do our beliefs about ourselves influence our communication?

4. What important information do our feelings give us?

5. How can listening and giving feedback help us identify each other's goals?

6. What are some roadblocks to couple communication?

7. What is vertical communication? Why does vertical communication often lead to discouragement?

8. What is level communication? In what areas of your relationship do you practice level communication? In what areas do you feel the need for level communication?

Activity for the Week

Continue Daily Dialogue and Encouragement Meetings.

For your Encouraging Days this week, make a new list of encouraging behaviors. The list can contain some of your original ideas, but you may wish to revise ideas or add new ones.

1. The family atmosphere in which you were raised influences the way you communicate in your marriage.

2. Beliefs and assumptions affect communication. Positive beliefs about yourself and your partner will help you improve your communication.

3. Feelings give energy to communication.

4. To fully understand what is being communicated we must be aware of feelings, beliefs, and goals or intentions.

5. An attitude such as "I'm right" or "It's your problem" can be a roadblock to communication.

6. When we practice level communication, we seek to understand, to negotiate, to encourage, and to reveal feelings.

7. When we communicate on a level, equal plane, we demonstrate that we accept responsibility for our own behavior and that we are sensitive to our partner's feelings.

8. Our communication improves when we become aware of the entire message we are communicating.

MY ◆ PLAN

Ways I can encourage _____

_____

Strengths I can use to improve the relationship _____

_____

Ways I can show I care or appreciate _____

_____

Ways I can improve my communication _____

_____

Effective ways I can resolve conflict _____

_____

I am ready and willing to change my behavior in the following way(s): _____

_____

MY PROGRESS IN APPLYING THESE SKILLS	I am doing this more	I need to do this more	I remain about the same
Listening to feelings			
Communicating honestly			
Encouraging			
Daily dialogue			
Communicating love			
Encouragement meetings			
Marriage meetings			
Resolving conflict effectively			
Demonstrating specific caring behavior			
Choosing a better marriage			
Spending time with my partner			

We often *say* what our partner wants to hear,
but our nonverbal behavior may convey
what we *really* feel and think.

CHAPTER SIX

Communication Skills

Have you ever heard someone say, "I just can't communicate?" Actually, each behavior we choose communicates—our words, our body language, our silence, and innuendo as well. When we say "I just can't communicate," we could more accurately say, "I'm just not getting my message across." We are feeling frustration from not being understood. In our marriage relationship it is vital that our partner understands what we are communicating.

Nonverbal Communication

A woman looks at her husband who is wearing a new, expensive suit for the first time. Her forehead is wrinkled with a frown. In a monotone voice she says, "That really looks good on you." What message is the woman communicating? Are her words said with sincerity or sarcasm?

Words are only a part of the total message we send. A gesture, a smile, a glare, a raised eyebrow, a touch are all ways of expressing ourselves. In the above situation, the woman seems to lack enthusiasm, but this may be her typical way of responding even when she is enthusiastic. Her husband may understand her message because he knows her well and accepts her outward lack of enthusiasm. Frequently, however, our nonverbal behavior detracts from the actual words we choose.

More than 70 percent of communication is nonverbal. If a message is misunderstood, our nonverbal behavior may be at fault. Become aware of the nonverbal messages you are sending through your tone of voice, gestures, facial expressions, eye contact, and posture. To become more sensitive to the nonverbal messages communicated between you and your partner, take five minutes to do the following exercise.

Sit face to face and begin a discussion in which you send a verbal message but at the same time intentionally send a different nonverbal message. For example, you might say while frowning, "I enjoyed the movie." Or, you might say in a very angry tone of voice, "Sure, I don't mind watching the kids while you shop." This exercise will help you become aware of what you are communicating through your nonverbal behavior.

Our nonverbal behavior at times may seem to contradict the message in our words. It is possible that our nonverbal message is the accurate message. Our nonverbal behavior may be conveying what we actually feel and think, but the words we choose are words that we feel our partner wants to hear. In this case, attention to our nonverbal behavior gives us clues regarding our true feelings.

Effective Communication

We do not necessarily communicate effectively just because we live together. To learn to communicate more effectively and to understand clearly what our partner is communicating to us requires skills. We begin with the desire to establish better communication in our marriage and the attitude that our communication can be improved.

Effective communication requires these skills:

- become aware of your true feelings and thoughts and share your awareness
- share feelings in an open, caring way by stating what you feel without blaming
- share meanings to be sure you understand each other
- share intentions

- affirm positive feelings by expressing ways you accept and value each other
- give positive feedback
- communicate negative thoughts and feelings in a caring manner

Sharing Awareness

Before you can express what you believe and feel honestly, fully, and accurately, you must cultivate awareness. Be sensitive to what you are experiencing so that you are able to share your perceptions, ideas, intentions, and feelings.

Awareness allows you to learn to speak for yourself. When you say, "Pam feels you neglect her," you mean "I believe Pam often feels you neglect her." Rather than saying, "Our social life is too limited," you say, "I don't feel our social life is as active as I'd like it to be."

When you communicate your awareness, begin with "I . . ." By using words that refer to yourself you indicate that you are sharing how you perceive and experience life events. For example, you say, "I would like to go on a vacation this summer," rather than "We never seem to get around to planning a vacation." Or, "I think you're not being firm enough with Jackson," rather than, "Do you think Jackson is really responding to the rules you set for him?" By using words that refer to yourself (I and me) you indicate that you are sharing how you perceive and experience life events. By sharing your awareness, you create an opportunity for discussion. Become aware of what you are feeling and then clearly communicate the feeling. The following examples illustrate the process of sharing your awareness.

Situation/Feeling	Communication of Awareness
You are displeased with the condition of the garage.	"I'm annoyed because by my standards the garage is a mess."
You are annoyed with the lack of variety in your social life.	"I feel bored because going to the movies every weekend is not stimulating for me."

Become aware of a feeling you have in one of the following areas. *How might you communicate your awareness?*

Area	Situation/Feeling	Communication of Awareness
Work around house	_____	_____
	_____	_____
Sexual relationship	_____	_____
	_____	_____
Social life	_____	_____
	_____	_____
Cooperation	_____	_____
	_____	_____
Common purposes and goals	_____	_____

Awareness allows you to learn to
speak for yourself.

Sharing Feelings

Your inner emotional experiences are communicated to your partner when you share your feelings. Sharing feelings makes it possible to work on solutions to problems in your relationship. If you and your partner have been unaccustomed to sharing feelings, this sharing may initially provoke defensiveness or aggressive responses. If you feel that you want to defend yourself or retaliate, remind yourself to listen empathetically and patiently. It takes time to learn to communicate openly and honestly.

When you share feelings, use statements rather than questions. Make a definite statement such as "I'm really pleased with your new schedule," rather than "I feel happier lately." Or, "I'm lonely when you're not here," rather than, "I'm feeling so lonely." Definite statements show that you are taking responsibility for your feelings. When a person chooses to ask questions or make general rather than definite statements it suggests that the person fears rejection and is, therefore, being very careful. It takes courage to reveal how we feel.

Fear and insecurity block the way to communicating what we are really feeling. When we hide our feelings, we sacrifice honesty and a chance to work toward common goals. Until we reveal who we are and what we feel, we cannot grow as individuals or marriage partners. Sharing feelings takes courage and causes us to risk rejection, but it is worth the risk and necessary in order to develop a deep, meaningful relationship.

How do you express your feelings?

Do you ask a lot of questions and give opinions rather than reveal how you feel?

Are your conversations general or do you share on a personal level?

Do you avoid intimacy by not sharing feelings?

It takes time to learn to communicate
openly and honestly.

Sharing Meanings

We interpret another person's message in light of our own experiences. Therefore, in order to understand what is communicated we must continually clarify what we mean and share what another person's message means to us. For example, your partner says, "We should plan to go to a movie." Your response might be, "I noticed a good one downtown. How about going this evening?" Your partner may have been expressing a general interest in seeing a movie. However, you were ready to act on the idea. Without clarification, what your partner expressed out of general interest can easily be misinterpreted as something to be done now. If you frequently interpret your partner's general statements in this manner, your partner may become hesitant in expressing ideas.

Always check out with your partner whether your interpretation of what was communicated is accurate. Listen to your partner's tone of voice, and notice other nonverbal clues. Clarify what you mean if it is apparent that your partner's interpretation seems inaccurate.

To practice sharing meanings, express your thoughts about one of the following topics.

Topic	Thought You Can Communicate
Vacation	"I like the idea of going to California next summer. I've always wanted to see the Pacific Ocean."
Future plans	"I think it's a great idea for you to think seriously about a career change. You have wanted to do something different for a long time."
Work	_____
	_____
	_____
Marriage	_____
	_____
	_____
Friends	_____
	_____
	_____

Sharing Intentions

To share intentions is to let your partner know what you want for yourself within your relationship. Intentions can be expressed by making "I"

HOW ABOUT A TIME OUT FOR THAT IMPORTANT PERSON IN YOUR LIFE?

Let your partner know what you want for yourself within your relationship.

statements, such as "I want . . ." "I prefer . . ." "I'd like to . . ." "I will be . . ." "I intend . . . ."

When we fail to express our intentions clearly and directly, we create a great deal of confusion and misunderstanding because our partner doesn't understand our desires or disappointment. Here is a situation in which a partner might be confused:

Mel: "I know you'd like to take a trip to your mother's this weekend, and it's possible I could do it. But if we don't go, maybe we could go the following weekend."

Mel's partner is not sure whether Mel plans to go, is unable to make definite plans, or prefers not to go. Mel could clarify his intentions in the following way:

Mel: "I know you want to go to your mother's this weekend. I'd enjoy that too. But I have a lot of things to do this weekend that can't be put off. I'd be happy to go with you next weekend."

In Mel's second statement he demonstrates awareness and acceptance of his partner's feeling, and at the same time he clearly indicates his own needs and intentions, leaving no unanswered questions in his partner's mind. The communication is clear and promotes understanding.

In order for your partner to understand you and to respond, you must state your intentions clearly. Otherwise you may think your partner is working against you when in fact your intentions are unclear. Here are examples in which intentions have been identified and stated clearly:

There are many opportunities to share positive feelings.

Intention	Communication of Intention
To be more involved with each other.	"I want us to do more things together."
To eat out without breaking a diet.	"I'd like to go where there's a good salad bar."
To be more involved in a religious community.	"I plan to go to church more regularly."
To become more physically fit.	"I intend to exercise every other morning."

What are your intentions in one or more of the following areas?

Topic	Your Intention	Communication of Intention
My leisure time		
Our budget		
Our sexual relationship		
Our social life		
My work		

Affirming

The process of affirming each other is vital in developing good communication in a marriage. By affirming what is positive about your partner and your marriage, you communicate acceptance and love. Your positive statements provide feedback that builds self-esteem. When we affirm, we focus on the positive. To affirm your partner, identify your partner's assets and notice any positive movement. Find a time to talk about things you value about each other and your marriage. The encouragement meeting provides a regular opportunity to affirm each other. When you are in the habit of affirming each other, you will find many opportunities and reasons to share your positive feelings.

The following phrases are useful in helping you to focus on what is positive:

"I like . . ."
"I appreciate . . ."
"I enjoyed . . ."
"I value . . ."
"I respect . . ."

Feedback

When you state what you are experiencing, without making a demand for change, you create greater certainty in your marriage. Feedback can be pleasant or unpleasant. The challenge is to let your partner know what you are experiencing without judging, criticizing, or complaining. The following examples illustrate how feedback can be given in a critical or noncritical way.

Critical Feedback

"You expect me to do everything."

Noncritical Feedback

"When you don't offer to help, I get the feeling you are unwilling to assume any responsibility at home."

Think of situations in which you might give your partner feedback. Identify a critical and a noncritical way of giving feedback.

Topic	Critical Feedback	Noncritical Feedback
Work		
Social life		
Leisure time		
Parenting		

Many husbands and wives are quick to recognize areas of dissension and slow to see opportunities to provide the positive feedback that will create a happier relationship. Although there are situations in which we must provide unpleasant feedback in order to be honest and open, it is important to identify areas in which we can give frequent positive feedback as well.

Understanding Feelings

When partners share feelings, ideas, and beliefs, our responsibility is to be attentive, respectful, and accepting. We demonstrate sensitivity by listening attentively in order to understand our partner's frame of reference. Earlier we discussed the skills of empathy. To be empathic, you will recall, we listen and observe attentively, not only to hear the words that our partners express, but also to understand the feelings expressed. We focus on nonverbal clues as well, such as tone of voice and gestures. By listening empathetically, we are able to identify with our partner's perceptions, thoughts, and feelings.

Our nonverbal and verbal behaviors assure our partners that we want to understand the message. By maintaining eye contact, by focusing on what is being said, and by giving feedback regarding our understanding of the message, we communicate caring and acceptance.

Empathy allows us to enter our partner's perceptual world and to spontaneously feel what our partner feels. Empathy may not result in agreement, but it allows us to demonstrate understanding. If we are empathic, our partner is more likely to reveal feelings and perceptions. Through sharing our deepest feelings, our relationship is enriched.

What do you do when your partner does not understand you or your feelings or when your points of view are incompatible? If you observe yourself in these situations, your behavior will help you measure your empathy.

The following exercise will give you practice in behaving empathetically:

1. Identify an issue or an area that is difficult for you to discuss with your partner.
2. Examine the issue from your partner's frame of reference. Can you identify the attitudes, feelings, and values that your partner holds regarding the issue?
3. Discuss the issue from your partner's point of view for 3-5 minutes.
4. What was it like to feel or think like your partner?
5. Now reverse roles and examine the issue from your own point of view. What are your feelings and beliefs regarding the issue?
6. Discuss the issue from your own point of view for 3-5 minutes.
7. Evaluate how the role reversal helped you.

Marriage Meeting

Listening, expressing feelings, getting feedback, and clarifying your own meaning are vital communication skills that will help you achieve satisfying agreements and accurate understanding of each other.

A marriage meeting provides an opportunity to put communication skills into practice in a systematic and caring way. With its emphasis on equal participation and equal responsibility, the marriage meeting provides a time and place for a couple to make decisions and solve problems. The meeting provides a setting for putting into action the marriage enrichment skills that you have learned. When a couple regularly schedules marriage meetings, they make a strong statement about the importance of their marriage.

If you believe you are too busy to find time to hold a marriage meeting, that may be the exact reason why you should have one. It is not enough to be aware of your partner's concerns and complaints. You need to be involved in helping your partner resolve such concerns. The marriage meeting allows for clarification of values, beliefs, goals, problems, and feelings. You can learn to work together setting policies, planning, and recognizing the pleasant as well as unpleasant aspects of your relationship.

Begin by following the suggested format for marriage meetings. Later you may wish to modify the format to meet your special needs. However, it is recommended that you not vary the format in the first two or three meetings.

Schedule a regular time, free of interruption, to hold a marriage meeting.

Guidelines for Marriage Meetings

1. Meet regularly at a time when you will not be interrupted. Schedule a minimum of 40 minutes for the meeting.

2. Prepare an agenda for the meeting. Each partner lists items for discussion. Post the agenda prior to the meeting. Keep meeting agendas in a notebook. Items to be discussed may relate to the topics indicated in the agenda format that follows:

Suggested Meeting Agenda

Positive things I like.

Discussion of work and chores.

Plans for fun.

Problems and challenges.

---

3. Participate as equals. Speak congruently, honestly. Listen empathetically.

4. Keep the meeting within established time limits.

5. Plan an activity to be shared that each of you enjoys.

6. Spend part of the time encouraging each other, pointing out what is positive and what is going well.

7. Avoid highly controversial subjects in the early meetings.

8. Make decisions jointly. Both partners must agree for a decision to be acted upon. If there is no agreement, defer the decision and action. The necessity of reaching consensus reinforces the importance of equality and partnership. The consensus procedure helps build a feeling of harmony, cooperation, and togetherness.

9. Plan time when you will agree to do things for each other that indicate caring. Exchange lists of things to do that indicate caring.

10. Prevent meetings from becoming primarily sessions for griping or arguing. Hear gripes and permit ventilating, but identify specific issues and develop positive suggestions. Use conflict resolution procedures when necessary.

11. Assess progress regarding decisions made at earlier meetings.

Most items on the agenda can be discussed in a conversational manner, within the guidelines suggested above. Discussion of problems and challenges, however, requires greater structure to be most effective. One partner begins by addressing a topic on the agenda, using no more than five minutes. The other partner then takes no more than five minutes to empathetically summarize feelings, beliefs, and perceptions heard. The partner who first spoke then takes no more than five minutes to clarify any part of the message, or acknowledges that the message was understood by the listening partner. When the message is clear the partners hold an open discussion of the issue in question, sharing opinions. When alternatives have been considered, the partners either reach consensus regarding future action or the topic is postponed. Then a new issue is introduced by the other partner. A portion of the marriage meeting should be devoted to the process of encouragement.

You are advised to follow the guidelines carefully until the format is well understood. By systematically following the guidelines and regularly scheduling marriage meetings, you and your partner will put into practice powerful communication skills that will enrich and energize your relationship. Through expressing and listening to words and feelings, you can grow to know each other more intimately.

Questions

1. What are some nonverbal ways we communicate?
2. How can you increase your awareness and your ability to share your awareness?
3. Why is it important to make definite statements when you are expressing feelings?
4. How do we share meanings? Give an example.
5. What is meant by sharing intentions? Give an example.
6. What do we do when we affirm another person? How can you affirm your partner?
7. How does empathy improve a relationship?
8. What are the guidelines for marriage meetings? What did you learn from your marriage meeting?

Activity for the Week

Continue Daily Dialogue and Encouragement Meetings.

Hold a Marriage Meeting. This week evaluate the meeting in terms of the *process*. A clear understanding of the process will ensure that future meetings will be most beneficial in helping you enrich your marriage.

Write and deliver a love letter to your partner.

1. More than 70 percent of our communication is nonverbal.

2. Our nonverbal behavior can help us understand our feelings or our partner's feelings.

3. We can develop skills that help us to communicate effectively and to understand what our partner is communicating.

4. To communicate honestly, fully, and accurately we must first develop awareness of our ideas, intentions, and feelings.

5. When we share our feelings, ideas, and intentions, we speak for ourselves. We can communicate our awareness by using "I messages."

6. When we share perceptions and feelings with our partners, it is important to get feedback and to give feedback.

7. Feedback helps us know if we understand and, in turn, if we are being understood by our partner. Let your partner know what you are experiencing without judging, criticizing, or complaining.

8. Empathy allows us to demonstrate understanding. If we are empathic our partners are more likely to reveal feelings and perceptions.

9. The marriage meeting provides an opportunity to put communication skills into practice in a systematic, caring way.

MY ◆ PLAN

Ways I can encourage _____

_____

Strengths I can use to improve the relationship _____

_____

Ways I can show I care or appreciate _____

_____

Ways I can improve my communication _____

_____

Effective ways I can resolve conflict _____

_____

I am ready and willing to change my behavior in the following way(s): _____

_____

MY PROGRESS IN APPLYING THESE SKILLS	I am doing this more	I need to do this more	I remain about the same
Listening to feelings			
Communicating honestly			
Encouraging			
Daily dialogue			
Communicating love			
Encouragement meetings			
Marriage meetings			
Resolving conflict effectively			
Demonstrating specific caring behavior			
Choosing a better marriage			
Spending time with my partner			

Partners may avoid making choices
unless a crisis forces a decision.

CHAPTER SEVEN

Choice in the Marital Relationship

Throughout our lives we have countless opportunities to choose. We make some choices consciously and others unconsciously. We permit certain choices to be made for us. Not all choices are of equal importance in creating our health and happiness. Nor are we always aware of the areas in which we can make choices. We sometimes confuse what happens by choice with what happens by chance. Even when we recognize areas in which we can make choices, we often find it extremely difficult to make those choices.

Why is it so difficult to make choices? We worry that we lack necessary information. Or we are afraid to act until we feel confident. We are often uneasy about giving up the known for the unknown because of an underlying fear of making a mistake. In our uncertainty, we may avoid making choices unless a crisis forces a decision. Fear and uncertainty turn choice-making into a chore rather than an opportunity to shape and control our lives.

Unfortunately, when we avoid making conscious choices, we have in effect made a choice to keep our relationship as it is. *Avoidance is acceptance.* By not choosing, we lose the opportunity for positive change. Even if we choose to maintain a relationship as it is, it is healthier for this to be a conscious choice rather than the result of avoiding a decision.

Your marriage today reflects the choices you have made since your marriage began. By your choices you create and maintain the marriage relationship you desire. Your marriage relationship is the way you really want it to be or it is what you have settled for. Whether or not you are satisfied with your marriage, you have chosen the quality of your relationship by your past decisions. There-fore, it is vital to understand the process of choosing.

In this chapter we will examine the choice-making process to help you identify areas in your marriage relationship where you can exercise the power of choice. You can refashion your marriage by making well-considered choices. By learning how to make choices with skill and purpose you can begin to direct your marriage toward the goals you desire.

The Process of Making Choices

Our understanding of the process of choosing begins with an awareness of the many areas of life in which we have opportunities to choose. Research indicates that what we say, how we feel, what we think, and how we act are all choices. When we are aware that we have control over so many choices, the discouragement we have felt in the past about our marital relationship can be replaced with hope. We can choose to be different!

In Chapter 1 you prepared a list of goals for your marriage. Refer to your list as you read this chapter to help you focus on areas in which your choices can help you begin to create the marriage you want.

In addition to becoming aware of areas in which we can choose, we must also learn to identify the *instant* when we can exercise our power to choose. If we are unaware of our moment of choice, we respond out of habit rather than as a result of having considered our options. Following every situation, or stimulus, there is an instant when we decide. By learning to identify the instant when a decision is possible, we can begin to make conscious choices that are in line with our goals. Many individuals believe that they are unable to make instantaneous discriminations. They may say, "I have no control over my anger," or, "When our schedule gets too full I always panic." When we hear ourselves making similar statements, we can ask ourselves, "Would I be able to control my response if I were in another setting such as at work or at church rather than in the security of my own home?" By identifying the moment of decision, we can take the opportunity to respond in a kinder, more caring, or more assertive manner regardless of where we are and who we are with.

In our marriage relationship we have the power to make harmful choices that restrict the marriage or helpful choices that encourage the development of a better relationship. Harmful choices include not listening, disregarding or breaking agreements, and abusing each other physically or verbally. Helpful choices include encouraging, helping with a chore, or demonstrating affection. It is important to increase the frequency of helpful choices and to eliminate harmful choices. We can enrich our marriage by choosing love and concern, by choosing to be assertive, by choosing fun, by choosing to be challenged, and by choosing to be congruent.

We must learn to identify the instant when we can exercise our power to choose.

Choosing Love and Concern

Choices that demonstrate that we care for our partner are always available to us. At times we can initiate caring behavior, and at other times we can choose to respond to our partner's demonstration of caring. Developing skills in demonstrating caring and responding to caring strengthens relationships. There are countless opportunities each day to show your partner that you care. Caring can be demonstrated by holding, touching, listening, assisting with projects, and comforting. Caring can be expressed verbally or nonverbally by smiling, nodding agreement, or by making statements or asking questions that make our caring apparent, such as "How are you feeling today?" or "You look tired. Why don't you take a nap?" or "Is there something I can do for you?"

List three ways you can choose to show more love and concern for your partner. Decide when you will begin.

_____
_____
_____

List three ways you would like your partner to show more love and concern for you.

_____
_____
_____

Choosing to be Assertive

Partners demonstrate responsibility in a marriage by choosing to be assertive. Assertive choices include making requests or suggestions, expressing opinions, or clarifying what we believe are our rights. When we make assertive choices, we demonstrate leadership. Assertive statements clearly express our position or wishes. The following expressions are examples of assertive statements: "Let's go to the movies tonight. I'll call the sitter." "Will you call me at 1 p.m.?" "Please stop by the grocery store on your way home and pick up some milk." "Stop! I'm feeling pushed and I need a minute to think."

List three ways you can choose to be more assertive in your marriage. When will you begin?

_____
_____
_____

List three different ways your partner can choose to be assertive with you.

_____
_____
_____

Choosing Fun

By choosing to be more spontaneous, we allow ourselves more opportunities for choosing fun. We tend to have a limited view of what is fun to do together. By becoming more spontaneous, we can develop our skills in choosing fun. We do have time for fun choices, and by choosing fun we may discover the most effective means for changing our marriage relationship in a positive way. By choosing fun we become more playful, loving, and creative.

Name three ways you can choose to have more fun with your partner. When will you begin?

_____
_____
_____

By choosing fun we become more playful, loving, and creative.

Choosing to be Challenged

We can choose to see marriage problems as challenges that require responsible action. When we choose to be challenged we work on our marriage relationship as vigorously as we attend to our employment or homemaking responsibilities. We choose to work, think, wonder, plan, and act to build a happier relationship.

List three problem areas in your marriage that you can choose to view as challenges that require action. When will you begin to act on these challenges?

_____
_____
_____

Choosing to be Congruent

When we choose to be congruent, we express our thoughts and feelings openly and honestly in constructive ways. When we are sad, hurt, or worried, we may choose to deny our feelings. Choose instead to be straightforward, acknowledging your feelings to yourself and to your partner. Choose to say, for example, "I feel sad when I hear my parents arguing with you," or "I worry that you cannot handle two jobs," or "It hurts when we can't work out our problems together."

Name three ways you can choose to be congruent. When will you begin?

_____
_____
_____

Important Choice-making Skills

1. Learn to identify the instant when you have the possibility to choose.
2. Clearly identify what you want to achieve.
3. Identify your alternatives and assess the potential gains and drawbacks of each. Develop the habit of asking yourself, "What are my options? Are there any choices I might have overlooked?" Or, "If somebody offered me $100,000 to discover another solution, could I?"
4. Make choices that allow you to make maximum use of your strengths and abilities.

5. Become aware of how your choice will affect you, your partner, and others. How are your choices influenced by other people and other factors? Will this choice be helpful or harmful to your marriage?

6. Make your choice and assume responsibility for making the choice work.

7. Remember, a choice can be changed.

You can apply these skills to the process of choosing your words, thoughts, feelings, and behaviors. Train yourself to be aware of the opportunity to choose. Put some time between the awareness that you can choose and the actual choice so that you can act rather than react. Although there is no guarantee that your conscious choice will produce the results you desire, you will gain information that in the future will help you eliminate choices that do not help you reach your goals. On the other hand, when you act out of habit rather than by choice, you may have little understanding of what is keeping you from reaching your goals.

Choosing Your Words

Any long-standing relationship is characterized by certain habitual ways of responding. In a marriage relationship, a couple may fall into the habit of giving little attention to what they say to each other. Because we have higher expectations of satisfaction in our marriage relationship, there is more to gain and more to lose as a result of our choice of words. If we respond out of habit rather than by choice, we lose many opportunities to encourage each other. Much tension and dissatisfaction in a marriage results from what we say or fail to say to each other.

In a marriage relationship the partners may choose words or phrases that have an automatic positive or automatic negative effect. We refer to such words as buzz words or phrases. Positive words encourage; negative words discourage. Below are examples.

Negative, discouraging phrases

"Why don't you grow up?"
"It's always going to be like this!"
"You will never change."
"You really have it rough!"

Positive, encouraging phrases

"I love you."
"I need you."
"Your_____ really turns me on."
"How can I help?"

List the words and phrases that your partner uses that encourage you and those that discourage you. Exchange lists with your partner.

Choose to speak clearly and kindly to your partner. Choose positive words that reflect understanding. Choose words that are thoughtful and considerate. Decide now to choose to communicate in helpful ways.

In a marriage relationship, your choice of words can have an automatic positive or negative effect.

Choosing Your Thoughts

Any change in your relationship will require a change in the way you think about yourself, your partner, and your marriage. You may choose to see your marriage as exciting. You may choose to see your partner's strengths. You may choose to see your marriage as satisfying.

Choosing to regard a partner's behavior as positive increases the likelihood that a partner will behave that way. A positive and hopeful attitude is contagious and can quickly improve the level of satisfaction in a relationship.

Our thoughts about a situation help determine our behavior. For example, if you believe that you and your partner will have fun together when you go out for an evening, you probably will behave joyfully. Even your nonverbal behaviors will reveal your expectation, with more smiling, excitement in your voice, and sparkling eyes. If you expect conflict when you go out together you will be more cautious. Your nonverbal behavior may include a more serious facial expression and less attending to your partner. Because your behavior becomes a stimulus to others, your behavior will create a self-fulfilling prophecy—you will get just what you expected.

Marital satisfaction can be increased by replacing negative thoughts with positive ones. To counter negative attitudes you can consciously learn to signal each other when you are observing or feeling negativity. You can choose to comment on the negativity you are observing or feeling and at the same time include a supportive comment. For example, you can say "I know you can tell I don't agree, but I want you to know I care about you and I'll support you, whatever your decision is." Or, "You seem unhappy about something. I'm willing to listen if you want to talk about it. I care about what you think."

When you behave *as if* your marriage relationship is satisfying, you convey positive expectations. Consequently, your partner will respond to some degree in a positive way and your marriage will begin to reflect your positive expectations.

Choosing Your Feelings

Feelings seem to appear whether or not we want them. However, by becoming aware of what we are feeling, we have an opportunity to choose whether or not to communicate a feeling to others. In a marriage it is common for each partner to act out or express most feelings, including negative and destructive feelings. In our relationships beyond our marriage, however, we clearly demonstrate that we can choose whether or not to communicate our feelings. To improve our marriage relationship it is helpful to delay responding to a negative feeling until we are sure that our response is in line with our goals. Becoming aware of what we do before we do it requires self-discipline and patience. Positive feelings give energy to a relationship. Negative emotions such as jealousy, resentment, boredom, anger, hurt, apathy, loneliness, anxiety, and depression sap the energy we need to build a satisfying marriage.

To rechannel negative energy, learn to identify the purpose of a negative emotion. What do you hope to gain by the feeling? Think of an alternative way to reach your goal. For example, if you are fearful of continuing a conversation you can demonstrate that feeling either by withdrawing or by saying "I feel trapped and unable to think clearly. Can we talk about this later?" By recognizing and communicating your feeling, you keep your response to the feeling from interfering with your relationship. Your partner will be less likely to be confused or threatened by this response.

A major challenge in a marriage is learning to deal with anger. Many couples believe they can protect their marriage by holding back their anger. This may well be the biggest mistake a couple can make. When anger is suppressed it eventually resurfaces in a more destructive form. Suppressed anger builds until there is a destructive explosion, or creates a climate of constant complaining that may cause a gradual erosion of love. The fact that suppressed anger can be so destructive does not give couples license to express anger and hostility indiscriminately. The closer we are to someone the more skilled we must become in expressing anger constructively. Learn to accept responsibility for your anger as well as other negative emotions and find constructive ways to express such emotions. In Chapter 8 you will learn more about dealing with anger in a constructive way.

When negative emotions occur, delay responding to the emotion until you choose a response that is in line with your marriage goals. Often you will be able to decide to exchange your present feeling for a new feeling. Choose to interpret a situation as challenging rather than overwhelming. By choosing to be optimistic about your relationship, your optimism will create more positive feelings.

Choosing Your Behaviors

When changing behaviors, it is usually necessary to make planned choices. At first new behaviors may seem unnatural or phoney. Because most people want behavior to be comfortable, they will not continue new, uncomfortable behaviors unless a specific program is developed to support the behaviors.

Choosing to have regular encouragement meetings with your partner is an excellent way to begin changing marriage behavior. Review the process for encouragement meetings described in Chapter 2.

The exercise below is useful in reinforcing attempts to change behavior. It illustrates a way to create opportunities to behave *as if* your marriage is the satisfying relationship you desire.

Make a list of specific positive behaviors that you would like your partner to do. Exchange lists with your partner. A list might contain behaviors such as:

1. Call me and ask me out for a surprise lunch.
2. Give me a kiss and hug when I leave or return.
3. Prepare my favorite meal.
4. Sit next to me and hold my hand while we watch TV.

By taking responsibility for letting your partner know what will give you happiness, and by acting in ways that give your partner happiness, you are behaving as if your marriage relationship is what you want it to be. When you behave in new loving ways, new behaviors become familiar and new

feelings emerge that help you continue the behaviors.

Even small changes can improve a relationship.

Understanding Why You Chose Your Partner

Many of us would prefer partners who do whatever we want, who are everything we need, and who know when to leave us alone. There is nothing wrong with this wish as long as we realize that it is an impossible dream. Unfortunately, many people begin marriage with the unrealistic notion that this dream is possible. To build a satisfying marriage we must know what we can realistically expect of each other, and what is realistic to expect of each other will change over time. To understand why we frequently hold on to unrealistic expectations, it is helpful to identify the reasons that we chose our partner.

Love may seem to be blind, but it is rarely as blind as we imagine. In fact our reasons for choosing each other are complex. Our choice of a marriage partner is determined by many factors both conscious and unconscious, factors that relate to our personal identity. When we understand the motivations surrounding our choice of a partner, we gain insight into the expectations we had for our marriage. Then we are able to decide if these expectations continue to be realistic.

Psychologist Laura Singer has found the following questions to be helpful in exploring why you chose your partner. When you answer the questions, Dr. Singer suggests that you not stop at the first response. Probe deeper. See if you can ask one more "why?" for each question.

1. *What about your partner initially attracted you? Was it the way he or she looked or acted? Was it where you went, what you did or talked about on the first date?*

2. *In what ways did you feel you understood or had an immediate or intuitive rapport with your partner? Did you have similar problems, experiences, goals, interests, lifestyles, etc.?*

3. *In what ways did you feel your partner was unlike you?*

4. *If you could design an ideal you, what characteristics would you strengthen?*

5. *What aspects of yourself that you approve of does your partner allow or encourage you to exercise?*

6. *In what ways does your partner remind you of things you like about your mother or father?*

7. *In what ways does your partner remind you of things you don't like about your mother or father?*[1]

This exercise illustrates that your choice of partner was based on a great deal of information. You knew a lot more about each other than you realized. The process of choosing a partner is complex because information, beliefs, and values that escape our conscious awareness are involved in the choice. Your personal aims and expectations had a great deal to do with your choice. The personal aims and expectations that entered into your decision were reflections of influences from your past as well as factors influencing you at the time you married.

Influences of the Past and Present

For each of us there are significant individuals in our lives who influence us and whose influence is reflected in our life plan. Frequently we marry an individual who resembles another important person in our life. The similarity may lie in physical features, mannerisms, or certain character traits. We may prefer a marriage relationship in which we are treated as we were treated earlier by a person of the opposite sex who was significant in our life. Casual relationships, as well as relationships with individuals such as our parents, may influence our choice of mate.

Selection of a mate is also influenced by our thoughts and fantasies. The media and advertising in our present culture dictate for many people the attributes of the ideal mate. Ideals change as social conditions and fashion change. A good example is the concept of physical beauty. What we regard as beautiful is a subjective decision about what we like and enjoy seeing. But our perceptions are strongly influenced by the latest fashions and advertising campaigns.

Frequently we marry individuals who resemble an important person in our life.

Tastes or preferences are important in determining with whom we fall in love. Personal preferences reflect inner motivations of which we are never fully aware. People seem to know what they want, but they are largely unaware of their real goals and purposes. We play an important role in bringing about the behavior we expect and want from our partner. By understanding the role of past and present influences in our life, we gain insight into how our expectations emerged and why it is frequently difficult, though not impossible, to change our expectations.

In your courtship period you may have been attracted to your partner because of his or her meticulous attention to appearance. If you expect that your partner will always maintain these qualities it is unrealistic to begrudge the time that your partner uses to carefully dress for a social occasion. Similarly, if you chose your partner because of his or her sensitivity and understanding it is unrealistic to expect your partner to be extremely assertive when dealing with poor service in a restaurant or department store. If you recognize the reasons you chose your partner, you are more able to value what your partner brings to the relationship and to free your relationship of unrealistic expectations.

Changes in circumstances often make it impossible for partners to fulfill each other's original expectations. Monica was attracted to Hal because of his strong will and motivation. When Hal became seriously ill, Monica had to make major adjustments in her life. She had to assume the role of principal breadwinner, and she had to learn to rely on her own strength and judgment.

Children provide dramatic change in a marriage relationship. Martin was attracted to Kate because of her willingness to be very attentive to his needs. When Kate became a mother, much of her time was spent attending to the children's needs. The amount of time she had to attend to Martin's needs diminished. Martin's expectations were no longer realistic.

It could easily be argued that Hal and Monica and Kate and Martin began marriage with unrealistic expectations. Even though their expectations seem unrealistic from an outsider's viewpoint, they may work for them. However, when expectations remain even though circumstances have changed unhappiness may result.

A clear understanding of the expectations you had when your relationship began can help you find new ways to meet each other's needs and to cope with life.

Should I Choose Again?

Sometimes it appears easier to choose to cut existing marital ties rather than resolve to strengthen the ties you have. However, the task of choosing again will not be easier than making new choices in your present situation. You are the source of your happiness. If you are in an unloving relationship, you need not seek a new mate to arouse your feelings. You can choose to rediscover your present mate. Sometimes separation and divorce seem to be the only solutions to personal survival. However, many marriages that seem terminally incompatible can be transformed into satisfying relationships when partners choose to live more creatively. Your second choice of the same person may be a wise one.

References

1. Laura J. Singer, *Stages: The Crises that Shape Your Marriage,* (NY: Grosset & Dunlap, 1980), pp. 21-24.

Questions

1. Why do partners often avoid making choices unless there is a crisis?
2. What questions can you ask yourself if you are having difficulty identifying an alternative choice?
3. Why is it important to become aware of the *instant* in which you can make a choice?
4. Are there situations in your marriage in which you feel you have no choice?
5. Why is it important that partners choose to be assertive?
6. How can choosing fun enrich a marriage?
7. Why is it important to deal with anger?

8. Why did you choose your partner? Why do you think your partner chose you?

Activity for the Week

Continue Daily Dialogue, and hold Encouragement Meetings and a Marriage Meeting.

During the week, commit to two new ways that you will show more love and concern for your partner. Your choices could involve a change in thoughts, words, feelings, or actions.

1. Marriage provides the opportunity and necessity for making continuous choices. However, partners often have trouble making choices.

2. A choice is any behavior over which we have some influence or control.

3. When we delay making choices that can improve our marriage, we are in effect choosing to keep our marriage as it is.

4. Be realistic and honest with yourself and your partner when making choices. Make choices you can or will act upon.

5. Choices are helpful when they encourage the development of a better relationship and harmful when they restrict the marriage.

6. Marriages can be enriched when partners choose love and concern, choose to be responsible, choose fun, choose to be challenged, and choose to be congruent.

7. We begin marriage with certain expectations about what the marriage relationship will bring. Changes in circumstances often make it impossible for partners to fulfill each other's original expectations.

8. By exploring the reasons you chose your partner you will discover more about your partner, yourself, and your marriage.

MY ◆ PLAN

Ways I can encourage _____
_____

Strengths I can use to improve the relationship _____
_____

Ways I can show I care or appreciate _____
_____

Ways I can improve my communication _____
_____

Effective ways I can resolve conflict _____
_____

I am ready and willing to change my behavior in the following way(s): _____
_____

MY PROGRESS IN APPLYING THESE SKILLS	I am doing this more	I need to do this more	I remain about the same
Listening to feelings			
Communicating honestly			
Encouraging			
Daily dialogue			
Communicating love			
Encouragement meetings			
Marriage meetings			
Resolving conflict effectively			
Demonstrating specific caring behavior			
Choosing a better marriage			
Spending time with my partner			

No other relationship offers the same potential for conflict.

CHAPTER EIGHT

Conflict in Marriage

What are the odds that a couple can live "happily ever after?" Consider the obstacles. No other relationship offers the same potential for conflict. Because we interact with each other in almost every facet of our lives, we have ample time and opportunity to disagree. We express our negative feelings openly and often intensely. We hold unrealistic expectations of each other. Over the years we undergo continuous change, and our changing rarely happens at the same time. Is it surprising, then, that we find it difficult to reach agreement on even minor issues? And issues such as sex, in-laws, money, children, and division of labor produce unending potential for conflict.

The odds of living "happily ever after" are very low. However, if we recognize that conflict is inevitable, we can learn to regard conflicts as challenges to be dealt with as they occur. Change always presents an opportunity to grow, and we can increase our happiness by learning to deal with the inevitable conflicts that occur.

Sources of Conflict

Love will keep us together. Our marriage will be different. We will make each other happy. Children will make our marriage happier. These are a few of the myths about marriage that are part of our society. Love keeps partners together only as long as they continue to behave toward each other in loving ways. Partners contribute to each other's happiness, but they cannot ensure happiness. Children may increase *personal* happiness, but they may detract from *marital* happiness. Marriages are often happier before children arrive and after they leave home.

Our dream of living "happily ever after" is a myth. A more realistic view of marriage suggests that our marriage *may* be different, that love *may* keep us together, that we will be *one* important influence on our partner's happiness, and that we will be able to satisfy *some* of our partner's needs. It is possible to be both realistic and positive about the future of our marriage.

Much conflict in marriage is a result of unrealistic expectations. Some expectations—like the myths described above—are perpetuated by society and others we create ourselves. When our unrealistic expectations are not met, disillusionment and disappointment follow. Marriage "just isn't what it was supposed to be." To expect perfect unity is to suffer from a romantic illusion. Conflict develops when one partner's behavior does not match the other partner's expectations, and poor communication sustains the conflict.

Areas of Potential Conflict

Although there is no area of our lives together in which we are immune from potential conflict, marital conflict most commonly centers on the following major areas:

Money. How much money do we need? Who should make the money? How do we decide who spends the money? What do we purchase? How much money should we borrow?

Sex. How often do we have sex? When? Where? Who should initiate sex?

Work. Can both partners work? Who decides what job to take? How much work is too much?

Children. Should we have children? How many? When? What type of discipline should we use? What goals or hopes for the children do we share?

In-laws. With whose parents shall we spend holidays? How often and how long should we visit? How shall we deal with parental interference?

Religion. What church should we attend? How can we resolve our different religious backgrounds? What religion should be taught to the children? How often should we attend church? Should we pray at the dinner table?

Friends. Can we have different friends? What about friends of the other sex? How much time can we spend with our friends? Do I have to like your friends? What if I don't like them?

Alcohol and Drug Usage. How much shall we drink? When? Where? How much money should be spent on alcohol? Is alcohol or drug use adversely affecting our relationship?

Recreation. How much time shall we spend on recreation? Do we have to pursue recreation together? Where do we spend our vacations? How many trips should we take each year? Should we spend vacations alone or take the children with us?

Resolving Conflict: An Effective Process

The way a couple deals with conflict determines whether or not the conflict will be harmful to their marriage. Failure to deal with conflict constructively is the most powerful force in dampening marital satisfaction. Conflict may also be the most prominent cause of divorce. When conflict occurs it often tends to be repeated. Thus it is important to learn to handle conflict appropriately. Conflicts inevitably occur in *all* marriages. The following steps can be used to find effective solutions to marital conflict:

Step 1. Show Mutual Respect. Rather than the issue itself, the attitude of one or both partners is often at the heart of the conflict. In a relationship with mutual respect each partner seeks to understand and respect the other's point of view.

Step 2. Pinpoint the Real Issue. Most couples have difficulty identifying the *real* issue. Who does what

around the house, how money is spent, or whether or not to have sex usually are not the real issues. These disagreements do have to be resolved, of course. But the purpose or goal the partner is trying to achieve is the real issue. Once the real issue is identified it becomes easier to resolve surface disagreements. The concern usually centers around one of the following issues:

1. You are feeling a threat to your *status* or *prestige.* "Why should I give in?" or "What will they think?"

2. You feel your *superiority* is being challenged. "If I'm not on top, I feel inadequate."

3. Your need to *control* or your right to *decide* is at stake. "If I don't boss them, they won't do it right" or "Why should I let him/her decide for me?"

4. You feel that your *judgment* is not being considered and you are being treated unfairly. "Whose way is the best way?"

5. You feel *hurt* and need to *retaliate* or *get even.* "S/he won the last one" or "I'll get even this time."[1]

When the issue has been identified—such as who controls, who resents control, who feels a lack of respect—the couple can discuss alternative ways to behave, and reach a new agreement.

YOU KNOW... MAYBE IF YOU WERE A VEGETARIAN, THINGS WOULD BE BETTER FOR US.

Most couples have difficulty identifying the real issue.

Writing out responses to the following questions will help you pinpoint the real issue.

What are some of the problems that might be causing the conflict?

What do I think is wrong?

How might my perception be affecting what I see as the problem?

How might my life style or belief system (values, faith, goals, outlook, commitment) be contributing to the way I see the problem?

Is there something external to our marriage that might be the underlying source of stress and conflict?

Is my present stage in life related to the conflict?

State your conflict in three different ways. Then look for alternative solutions that are suggested by each new way you have defined the problem.

I said our conflict was _____

_____

Our conflict really is _____

Possible Solutions

a. _____

_____

b. _____

_____

c. _____

_____

Our conflict may be _____

_____

Possible Solutions

a. _____

_____

b. _____

_____

c. _____

_____

Or perhaps it is _____

_____

Possible Solutions

a. _____

_____

b. _____

_____

c. _____

_____

Step 3. Seek Areas of Agreement. In a conflict situation, the most comfortable solution that comes to mind is to suggest how our partner could change to alleviate the problem. A more effective approach is to ask, "What can *I do* to change our relationship?" By concentrating on what you are willing to do and by not requiring your partner to change, you create an atmosphere in which agreement can be reached. Although the ultimate solution to conflict involves mutual change of behavior, the desire and decision to change is the responsibility of each individual.

By agreeing to cooperate rather than bicker, a couple sets the stage for discovering what they can each do to resolve the conflict.

Step 4. Mutually Participate in Decisions. As partners work on a problem and the issue becomes clear, either may propose a tentative solution. A partner may respond by accepting the proposed solution, modifying it, or making a counter suggestion. An atmosphere of give-and-take is most effective. For example, "I would be willing to go dancing twice a month if you would agree to leave at midnight." When an agreement is reached, clarify the role of each partner in carrying out the decision and decide what should be done if either partner doesn't follow through.

It is important to allow a partner the option of not being involved in a decision, providing the partner was given a choice to be involved or uninvolved. Conflict may occur when a decision is made without giving a partner the option to be involved. For example, Cal bought a car and drove it home, expecting Barbara to be excited about his purchase. Barbara was surprised, but she was also annoyed. Cal was confused because Barbara had never expressed an interest in helping select a car in the past. However, Cal had always asked Barbara's opinion regarding when to buy a car and what color she would like. Because Barbara had not been consulted this time, she felt annoyed and left out and became resistant to the whole idea of the purchase. The fact that Cal purchased the car was not the real issue. The real issue was the way in which the decision was made. By giving each other the option to participate in the decision, the problem is eliminated.

When both partners mutually participate in conflict resolution, they can develop creative agreements that are acceptable to both and that are in line with their common goals. Responsibility and power are shared equally, and cooperation replaces resistance.

Conflict often occurs when important decisions are made by only one partner.

General Suggestions for Conflict Resolution

If you were to take a final test regarding the skills presented in this book, it would probably be announced in this way: "Sometime in the next week you and your partner are going to lock horns over some issue. Demonstrate what you've learned in this handbook." The necessity for empathic listening, the importance of practicing congruent communication, the need to encourage, the value of using "I messages"—all of these skills are called into action when you experience conflict.

The following suggestions relate the skills you have been learning specifically to the process of solving conflicts.

Be specific. Concrete facts and statements are easier to deal with than abstractions and generalizations. Being specific helps both partners clarify their thoughts and increases the chances of agreement.

Be present- and future-oriented. Learn to ask "How can we solve this problem?" rather than "Why do we have this problem?" Bringing up the past directs attention away from the challenges at hand. Replace "why" questions with "when," "what," or "how" questions.

Use active listening. Listen attentively. Active listening enables you to empathetically focus on the entire message that includes not only your partner's words but the underlying thoughts, beliefs, and feelings as well.

Use "I messages." Begin sentences with "I." By using "I messages," you tend to accept responsibility for your behavior rather than blame your partner.

Avoid absolutes. Statements that include "always," "never," "should," or "ought" as the second word tend to exaggerate the issue at hand and leave no room for human error. Avoid such statements.

Do not attempt to determine who is right and who is wrong. The goal in solving conflicts is to have the relationship win. In marital conflicts, both the winner and the loser are losers because a conflict is unresolved unless both partners are satisfied. Cooperation rather than competition is important.

Resolving the issue peacefully and equitably takes precedence over winning the battle.

Solutions are not forever. A solution need not be eternally binding. When solutions are seen as tentative, both partners are more willing to risk agreement. Make a firm commitment to the agreed-upon solution, try it out for a specific period of time, and then evaluate.

Solve one problem at a time. Some couples try to tackle too many problems at once, adding tension to the relationship when the desire is to reduce tension. Seek solutions in small steps. Be patient! Address specific issues one at a time.

Understanding is the goal. Mutual understanding is the goal of discussion. Agreement is impossible if our goal is to get the other person to change.

Our attitude determines the meaning we give to facts. Facts in themselves are neither good nor bad. We give our own meaning to the facts. We see what we want to see. We find what we expect to find. We arrange and interpret our experiences.

Watch for fouls and low blows. We all know what we can say to our partners that will stimulate a negative reaction. Avoid blaming. Avoid accusations.

Do it now. Time delays tend to add to resentment and confusion. Deal directly and openly with problems at the time they occur, or as close to the time as possible.

Optimize conditions. The time, place, and circumstances in which we try to resolve conflict influence the chances of reaching an acceptable solution. Make certain the conditions are supportive. If they are not, delay discussion while you work to improve the conditions.

Learn to recognize normal developmental crisis. Certain areas of conflict are predictable in different stages of marriage, such as birth of the first child, moving, job change, or an in-law's joining the household. Recognize that these are no-fault situations. Stress normally accompanies change, even if the change is pleasant and desirable.

Say what you are thinking and feeling. Say what you think or feel even when it might seem unrealistic or selfish. You may be surprised to learn that your partner is unaware of something you want.

We all know what we can say to our partners that will stimulate a negative reaction.

Don't expect your partner to read your mind. State your feeling or thought in a positive way, such as "I want you to excite and surprise me" rather than "I don't want our marriage to be so boring." If you're expecting guests in fifteen minutes and the house is a mess, ask for help instead of thinking that your partner ought to realize that you need help. Also, remember that just because you have said something in the past, you cannot expect your partner to remember it always.

Learn to change habitual responses. Recognize and eliminate destructive, nonproductive arguments. Stop fighting to win. Instead, consider and identify what your most frequent and intense confrontations are about. A compromise that works, even though not ideal, is better than a brilliant solution imposed upon a resentful partner. Winning does not bring happiness and peace. Solving conflicts does.

Stress normally accompanies change, even if the change is pleasant and desirable.

Set a limit on time spent discussing problems. Marriage should not be a continual round of discussion. There must be time for enjoyment and acceptance.

Allow time to change. Use consistent and persistent effort. Old habits supported by old ways of thinking require time to change. Patience is a virtue.

Ask yourself a new question when you can't find a solution. The following questions are helpful in getting beyond a stalemate in your discussion:

- *How did this impasse develop?*
- *What do you want from this discussion?*
- *How can you communicate what you want more effectively?*
- *Does your mate know that he or she is the most significant person in your life?*
- *How are you growing at this point in your marriage?*
- *Could you be limiting your partner's growth by sustaining this conflict?*

- *What is the worst possible thing that could happen if you don't resolve the conflict exactly as you want it resolved?*
- *Can you live with another decision?*
- *What is your underlying fear about this decision?*

Accept responsibility. Accept responsibility for your feelings and mistakes. Learn to monitor your level of stress and tension. We become angry and resentful toward those around us when we are angry with ourselves. Even when the source of pain seems to be your partner, reflect what is really going on inside yourself. What is the purpose of your emotion?

"I'd Rather Not Talk About It!"

A habit of avoiding conflict creates, at best, a false atmosphere of peace. Partners pay a high price for this kind of peace. There are marriages of long standing in which partners rarely discuss things that matter most to them. When conflict occurs some partners withdraw and refrain from saying anything. Others immediately change the subject or walk out in the middle of the discussion. Couples may consciously or unconsciously work to avoid situations in which they might have time

Couples may unconsciously avoid communicating.

to talk about anything other than their jobs, the bills, and the children. If she suggests, "Let's go out for dinner tonight," he promptly responds, "Good idea. I'll see if the Millers want to come along." If he says, "I was thinking it might be fun to go to the cabin this weekend," she says, "Great idea. I'll ask the McDonalds if they would like to come too."

On the surface, a relationship may appear to function smoothly. In reality, the couple may be terrified of true intimacy. The extent to which we will go to avoid discussion of conflicts may serve as an indicator of how much we fear rejection and hurt feelings.

Dealing With Anger

There is a high probability that married partners will experience anger more frequently in their marriage relationship than in any other relationship. To understand why there is such a high probability for anger in marriage, it is important to understand the reason for anger. Anger is a normal, necessary emotion basic to our survival. Anger occurs spontaneously when the brain interprets a situation as dangerous. Simply stated, anger is a signal that something is wrong. Anger should be regarded as a normal, necessary emotion that is capable of teaching us something about ourselves and our relationship. The question to ask is "What is my anger trying to tell me?"

Anger is often triggered by fear, frustration, lowered self-esteem, and hurt feelings. We have a great deal at stake in our marriage. We mean more to each other and therefore have the potential for hurting each other more deeply. More of our needs are met by our marriage relationship. We interact in more facets of our lives than in any other relationship. In short, marriage partners have the opportunity and the potential to evoke feelings of frustration, fear, and lowered self-esteem in each other—feelings that may result in anger.

Anger is an emotion that is basic to our ability to survive. When we feel angry, it is a signal like the squeak in your car motor that tells you that something needs to be fixed. If we pay attention to anger when it occurs and learn to deal with anger

in a constructive way, our marriage relationship will run more smoothly. If we ignore the anger or deal with it in a destructive way, our marriage relationship will suffer.

To allow anger to be a constructive force in a relationship we need to acknowledge that anger is an inevitable part of our lives together and learn a process for dealing with it when it occurs. Responding to our own anger by feeling guilty or ashamed is counterproductive.

How can we deal with anger? We can vent it, which generally means we fight back. We can suppress it by avoiding the issue. Or we can process it.

People who vent their anger operate from the belief that they must "express" their anger in order to get it out of their system. Venting is the "fight back" response. Ventors let all their aggressive feelings out, often with a bang.

When we choose to vent our anger we are saying to the body, "Keep the anger coming! The fight is still on." One way of venting anger is to vigorously exert tense muscles, a process that brings physical relief. For example, a person may try to "get anger out" by engaging in vigorous physical activity such as beating or kicking pillows. Such action may relax the tense muscles, but it doesn't deal with the anger. It may in fact be more effective to relax the muscles and thus communicate to the body that the crisis has passed.

A second way of responding to anger is to suppress it. This is the policy of avoiding the issue— peace at any price, or just forget it. When all difficult or painful situations are swept under the rug, nothing every gets openly and honestly settled. Suppressors bottle up their feelings until they sour and poison them inside.

For the health of our marriage relationship and for our personal well-being, a third way of responding to anger—to process anger—is the only alternative. Dr. David Mace suggests a four-step process in learning to deal with anger in your marriage. When you are experiencing anger, sit down with your partner and find the answers to four questions:

1. *What* situation *made me angry?*
2. *What do I* feel *when I get angry with you?*

3. *What do I* do *when I get angry with you?*

4. *What do I* wish *we could both do when we get angry with each other?*[2]

Even though only one partner is angry both partners have a responsibility to work through the anger together. What we are doing is acknowledging, "We got angry with each other, and we need to find out exactly why." By exploring thoughts and feelings a couple may identify the primary emotion—such as fear, frustration, lowered self-esteem, or hurt feelings—that produced the anger.

When you are angry it is important to tell your partner about your anger within twenty-four hours. Share your inner thoughts and feelings and ask for feedback from each other to make sure that the messages are being understood. Agree before sharing that you will not attack each other. When you are sure you have revealed your feelings openly and honestly, discuss options for dealing with the issue that seems to have triggered the anger. Decide on an option that you can act on, and check with each other regularly to see if you are making progress. If there are deep feelings that require more attention, follow through by planning a definite time to deal with the issue in your marriage meetings.

How do we know if our anger is related to a specific situation or if it is a signal that deeper feelings are the real issue? Ask yourself, "Do we deal with anger in one situation and find that almost immediately there is another situation in which anger surfaces?"

When a couple is able to share feelings, their intimacy allows them to feel secure enough in their relationship to reveal the hurt and fear of further hurt that may underlie the anger. Most of us have difficulty becoming aware of and expressing our feelings of hurt and fear of further hurt. In our society men find it more difficult to express sadness than to express anger. However, anger often signals the presence of hurt feelings. Women may be more quickly aware of feelings of hurt, but they, too, may have difficulty constructively expressing hurt feelings. For both men and women the hurt that underlies anger is often associated with unre-

solved grief, past frustrations and failures, feelings of inadequacy, and loneliness.

Until we uncover the hurt feelings and fear of further hurt that are resulting in anger, we may find that we deal with one situation that evoked anger only to see another one appearing almost immediately. Therefore, in marriages in which the relationship never seems to be rid of anger, dealing with a specific situation that resulted in anger is not enough. Until each partner comes to terms with the unresolved pain that is being expressed in anger, the anger will reappear. Intimacy—sharing feelings openly, and honestly, without fear—allows partners to work through the feelings.

Open dialogue is vital to a living marriage. Conflict is inevitable between two human beings who have totally different histories, belong to different sexes, and look at the world from different perspectives. The ongoing process of blending two personalities into a relationship that is mutually enriching involves effort and pain. To avoid the effort and the pain is to give up the intimacy that is the true substance of effective marriage. It is important to acknowledge that conflict is inevitable, and to be prepared to deal with it when it occurs.

References

1. Rudolph Dreikurs, Shirley Gould, and Raymond J. Corsini, *Family Council*, (Chicago: Henry Regnery Co., 1974).

2. David Mace, *Enriching Your Marriage*, (Waco, TX 76796: Word, Inc., 1980).

Questions

1. Name several unrealistic expectations about marriage. What unrealistic expectations do you have? What unrealistic expectations have you had in the past?

2. How do unrealistic expectations affect marital happiness?

3. How can conflict help a marriage grow?

4. In what areas of marital life are conflicts most common?

5. What are the four steps for resolving conflict?

6. How can couples identify the *real* issue behind their conflict?

7. Do you believe that anger can be used as a constructive rather than destructive force in a marriage? Why or why not?

8. Why is it important for both partners to deal with anger even though only one partner is angry?

Activity for the Week

Continue Daily Dialogue, and hold Encouragement Meetings and a Marriage Meeting.

Hold a meeting with your partner to work toward resolving a conflict. Use the four-step process:

Step 1. Show mutual respect.

Step 2. Pinpoint the *real* issue.

Step 3. Seek areas of agreement.

Step 4. Mutually participate in decisions.

1. Myths about marriage create unrealistic expectations in many marriages.

2. Conflict is an inevitable, necessary part of marriage.

3. The major areas of conflict in marriage are money, sex, work, children, in-laws, religion, friends, alcohol and drugs, and recreation.

4. The conflict resolution process involves four steps:
   a. Show mutual respect.
   b. Pinpoint the real issue.
   c. Seek areas of agreement.
   d. Participate mutually in decisions.

5. To resolve conflict, be specific and concentrate on the present and future rather than the past.

6. Effective communication skills are essential in resolving conflict.

7. Solve one problem at a time and realize that even the best solution may not be the solution needed forever.

8. Change takes time. Be patient with your progress.

9. If we learn to deal with anger in a constructive way our marriage relationship will run more smoothly.

MY ◆ PLAN

Ways I can encourage _____

_____

Strengths I can use to improve the relationship _____

_____

Ways I can show I care or appreciate _____

_____

Ways I can improve my communication _____

_____

Effective ways I can resolve conflict _____

_____

I am ready and willing to change my behavior in the following way(s): ____

_____

MY PROGRESS IN APPLYING THESE SKILLS	I am doing this more	I need to do this more	I remain about the same
Listening to feelings			
Communicating honestly			
Encouraging			
Daily dialogue			
Communicating love			
Encouragement meetings			
Marriage meetings			
Resolving conflict effectively			
Demonstrating specific caring behavior			
Choosing a better marriage			
Spending time with my partner			

Conflicts can be regarded as opportunities to grow.

Conflict Resolution: Applying Your Skills

Whenever conflict occurs, a couple has three choices: they may fight, avoid, or solve the problem. If they choose to fight, their energy is devoted to trying to establish who is right and who is wrong. The conflict remains unresolved. If they choose to avoid the issue, the conflict will surface again and it is likely to be more severe. Choosing to solve the problem is clearly the only wise alternative.

The severity of a problem is not the determining factor in whether the conflict will or will not be resolved. The willingness of the partners to deal with the issue is the key factor in conflict resolution. Any conflict has the potential to jeopardize a marriage. However, even the most severe problem faced together in an atmosphere of encouragement and cooperation can bring partners closer together and strengthen their marriage.

In Chapter 8 you were introduced to an effective conflict resolution process. In this chapter the process is applied to areas of the marriage relationship in which conflict most commonly occurs. Notice that the word *challenge* replaces the word *conflict* in the headings of each section as an ongoing reminder that conflicts can be regarded as challenges that present opportunities to overcome and grow.

The Challenge of Sex

A couple's sexual relationship is like a barometer, reflecting the highs and lows of the relationship. Sex tends to be the central symbolic area of life. The sex act—a comparatively simple matter—has become the most written about, the most talked about, and the most misunderstood aspect of marriage. Much of the excessive emphasis on sex and much resulting unhappiness can be attributed to myths that distort the role of sex in our lives.

Sex has become the most written about, the most talked about, and the most misunderstood aspect of marriage.

Myths	**Facts**
1. Sex is the same thing as genital intercourse.	1. Genital intercourse is only one aspect of sex. Sex is a part of our total being. Our sexuality is reflected in all of our actions.
2. A poor sexual relationship is a major cause of marriage failure.	2. Unsatisfactory sexual relations are one symptom of marital discord, not the cause. Evidence suggests that a person's perception of what represents a good sexual relationship is more important than the sex act itself.
3. Sex is best in a romantic relationship.	3. Sex is best in whatever type of relationship you desire.
4. Women have lower sex drives than men.	4. Research indicates that the female sex drive may be slightly higher.[1]
5. It is important for both partners to reach climax at the same time.	5. Mutual orgasm may be enjoyable but it is neither necessary nor always achievable. Due to different rates of excitation, mutual orgasm is the exception rather than the rule. Separate orgasms are just as satisfying as simultaneous orgasms.
6. The best marriages have no problems — especially sexual ones.	6. All couples experience problems, including sexual problems. The healthy couple works together to solve the problems.
7. Sex is simply doing what comes naturally. You don't need to discuss it with your mate, read books about it, or prepare for it.	7. Sex is a complex process that involves high levels of collaboration and communication.
8. Penetration is the beginning of sex and ejaculation the end.	8. Sex takes place all day.
9. Sex is serious business.	9. Sex may be playful, mysterious, or seductive, as well as serious.
10. Sex must be performed in certain ways.	10. People have been tricked into believing that sex must be performed alike by everybody. The so-called *standards* for sexual performance are established by advertising, literature, movies, plays, and television.

These myths perpetuate the idea that there is a single, absolute standard to be reached by all. Experts emphasize that there is no "normal" sexual relationship. Sexual expression varies greatly from one marriage to another, both in quality and quantity.

Sex Problems

Sex therapists follow the rule, "Treat the relationship before focusing on the sexual problem." This rule is based on the premise that the sexual relationship reflects the whole relationship between partners. What happens outside the bedroom in day-to-day interaction has a tremendous influence on what happens inside the bedroom.

The following questions may be helpful in pinpointing areas of your sexual relationship that either you or your partner consider to be problems:

1. *Are you pleased with the frequency of your sexual activity? Is your partner's interest in sex different from yours?*

2. *Do you feel that there is enough touching, kissing, and hugging in your relationship?*

3. *Can you talk freely about sex with your partner?*

4. *Can you ask for what you want from your partner in sex?*

5. *When something thrilling happens in sex, can you tell your partner about it? Something disappointing?*

6. *Do you feel comfortable initiating sex? Do you initiate sex half the time?*

7. *Are you able to share sexual fantasies with your partner?*

8. *Would you like to have more variety in sexual activities with your partner?*

The answers to your questions can serve as a basis for discussion between you and your partner. When you have identified specifically what you want to change in your sexual relationship, you are halfway toward finding a solution. When you want the salt at the dinner table you do not sit and wait, hoping someone will pass it. You speak up. Sexual relationships require the same clarity of expression. A marriage partner is not a mind reader.

An Example of Sexual Conflict Solution

Ron and Alice enjoy sexual relations. Ron likes to have sex often and fairly quickly. Alice also likes frequent sex, but she prefers a long period of romantic foreplay. The couple's arguments over this matter have resulted in total abstinence for both.

Step 1. Mutual Respect. In an emotion-laden situation involving sex, it is important to clearly understand and accept each person's point of view.

Alice: "I really enjoy being with you, and I love having sex. But it just isn't good for me unless we do it slowly."

Ron: "You don't have orgasms with me?"

Alice: "Not always."

Ron: "I do want to please you, but lots of foreplay is boring to me. I feel like I'm wasting my time."

Alice: "You don't like being with me?"

Ron: "I like being with you, but I don't like doing the same thing over and over."

Step 2. Pinpointing the Real Issue. Through clear communication, Ron and Alice can increase their understanding of the real problem. Ron apparently is resisting changing their format because he wants to control.

Alice: "I think you're just making up a reason to excuse yourself for not changing."

Ron: "You don't believe me?"

Alice: "It's not that I don't believe you, but it seems like every time we get into a conflict you come up with some reason to keep things the same."

Ron: "I guess I like to have the final word."

Alice: "I let you do it too. I don't very often tell you what I'm feeling."

Step 3. Seek Areas of Agreement. Ron and Alice agree on two issues: they both enjoy sex, and they both are contributing to the real problem.

Ron: "I don't like to admit it, but it does seem like I've been controlling you and our relationship. But I guess you've been covering up your feelings because until now I haven't gotten any clue about what's wrong."

Alice: "I didn't want to say anything to make you mad. I have been upset for quite a while."

Step 4. Mutual Participation. Ron and Alice seem to have developed accurate insight into their problem. It is now time to decide on action.

Alice: "I don't need to have long periods of foreplay all the time. How about if we have one long night of romance before sex each week?"

Ron: "That would be okay with me, as long as we plan it in advance."

Alice: "Let's choose on Sunday."

Ron: "Fine."

Use the conflict solution process to solve the following sexual challenge:

Julio and Elena have been married seven years. Julio is unhappy because he and Elena have sexual intercourse only twice a week. He asks Elena every day to "get together." Elena is mostly pleased with the frequency of their sexual relations, but can't stand the fights that go on when she declines. Because she feels that Julio won't accept her decision if she simply says "not tonight," she has developed an arsenal of excuses, such as headaches, fatigue, and being too busy.

Step 1._____

_____

Step 2._____

_____

Step 3._____

_____

Step 4._____

_____

The Challenge of Finances

"When the money got tight they started to fight" is a commonly heard lament. It sounds good, but it probably is not true. Although some marriages deteriorate under financial pressure, many marriages are strengthened. The Great Depression, for example, deepened some marital unions, while breaking others. Although economic problems often appear to have caused the collapse of a marriage, we often find deeper reasons. Sometimes the foundation of a marriage is not broad enough to withstand financial stress. In marriages already in the process of deteriorating from other friction, the slightest additional burden completes the destruction.

Money is a powerful influence on human behavior, and even though it may not be as significant a factor in destroying marriages as is commonly believed, money problems do cast a shadow on marital happiness. Usually there is not enough money. Or, the amount of time and energy that are invested in the pursuit of money leaves little time for the relationship. And when the money is earned the issue becomes, "How are we going to spend it?"

I DON'T THINK WE AGREE ON "WHAT GETTING BACK TO BASICS" MEANS.

Money problems cast a shadow on marital happiness.

The significance of money in our lives is enormous and highly complex. Money is a kind of bartering device that gives us control over other people and situations. Money can represent love when we spend it, power when we have it, and hostility when we withhold it. Unfortunately, money represents more than economic security to many people. Money is closely related to status and to our self-esteem. People who lack money may feel inadequate. When we confuse what we have with who we are, money affects our emotional security. As Hugh Prather points out, more than things what we really want is experiences, and money is not the *only* way to create experiences.[2]

Money problems are so common that some couples expect them to continue for a lifetime. Consciously or unconsciously many of us ensure the permanent presence of financial difficulties. Using credit cards indiscriminately, refusing to stick to a firm budget, going on a buying spree, gambling, overspending for housing, clothing, recreation, and furniture—all pave the way to serious financial problems.

An Example of Financial Conflict Solution

Bob and Dorothy have had a relatively stable marriage for six years. They are raising two lovely daughters and have recently made a down payment on a house. The house purchase, combined with inflation and hidden costs involved in raising a family, have left them in a serious financial dilemma. They must decide how to get the necessary money. Bob wants to take a part-time job in the evenings. Dorothy feels that she and the girls don't see enough of him now. She thinks she should go back to work. Bob doesn't like the idea because he wants her home with the girls. He feels he missed out on a lot because his mother had to work.

Step 1. Mutual Respect. It is important for both Bob and Dorothy to convey respect for each other's viewpoint.

Dorothy: "What do you think the girls will miss out on if I go to work?"

Bob: "I never liked coming home to an empty house. I don't want them to go through what I did."

Dorothy: "I could get a job that would allow me to be home before the kids."

Bob: "But what about the summers?"

Dorothy: "There are jobs in the school district or at the college that are only nine-month jobs."

Bob: "Boy, you must really want to work!"

Step 2. Pinpoint the Real Issue. Through clear communication it becomes apparent that Bob's sense of prestige is threatened by Dorothy's desire to go to work.

Dorothy: "I think the real problem with my working is your ego. If I go to work you'll feel as if you're not providing for us."

Bob: "I do feel it's my job to make the money and your job to take care of the house."

Dorothy: "I feel it's your job to be a good husband and father by being home as much as possible."

Step 3. Seek Areas of Agreement. Both Bob and Dorothy have agreed that their financial situation must be improved, but not at the expense of their family life. They have agreed to honestly discuss the problem. Both are willing to take on additional responsibility.

Step 4. Mutual Participation. There are many possible solutions to their problem. The important point is not the solution as much as whether *both partners are involved in the process.*

Dorothy: "Maybe we should look for work that we can do in our home. We could earn the necessary money and still have time together as a family."

Bob: "I'm not sure what kind of work you have in mind."

Dorothy: "Two of our neighbors sell some kind of household products. And a woman I met at church has a telephone answering service at home. I think if we gave it some thought and talked to people we could come up with something we'd like to do."

Bob: "I think it's a good idea if we can figure out something that doesn't take a lot of money to begin."

Dorothy: "I'll start getting some information tomorrow. I'll call you at work if I find something that looks good."

Use the conflict solution process to solve the following financial challenge:

Harry and Bess are both employed. Although they take home a good combined income they are unable to pay their bills each month. Bess feels the solution is for Harry to spend less money by taking a lunch to work instead of eating out. Harry thinks that Bess should give up her bowling league.

Step 1._____

_____

Step 2._____

_____

Step 3._____

_____

Step 4._____

_____

The following questions may be helpful in determining if finances are a problem in your marriage:

1. *Do you feel that your personal income is yours or belongs to the partnership? How do you regard your partner's income?*

2. *Does each partner have some separate money to spend freely?*

3. *If one person handles the bookkeeping, is it okay with the other?*

4. *Do you spend money when you are angry? Do you spend compulsively?*

5. *Do you feel guilty or bad when you spend money?*

6. *Do you and your partner often quarrel about money?*

7. *Have you and your partner agreed on a savings program?*

8. *Do you wish your partner would spend less money?*

The Challenge of Recreation

"We don't seem to have much in common anymore" and "We never do anything together" are frequent laments of couples. In the midst of the responsibilities of running homes, raising children, and going to work, it is a challenge for couples to figure out ways to be together and have fun. One of the reasons a man and a woman marry is because they enjoy each other. Although it's unrealistic to assume that there will be the same amount of time for fun later in marriage, it's equally unrealistic to assume that there is no time for fun. Marriage is not, after all, a business. Happy, meaningful relationships depend on setting aside time for regular play. A relationship suffers if the partners do not spend some of their play time together.

Shared activities contribute to continued enjoyment of and involvement with one's partner. When married people choose to spend all their time apart, they lose contact with one another, and feelings of closeness diminish. It is important to discuss whether you are both satisfied with the way you use your nonworking time. Explore together your ideas of what is fun. Do you share your partner's recreational interests? Do you both like to attend cultural events such as opera, ballet, symphony, and the theater? Do you like to watch sports events? What sports do you like to participate in? Do you have similar interest in sedentary activities such as going to movies, watching television, or reading? How do you feel about going to parties? Are you comfortable at either formal or informal parties? Does the use of alcohol or drugs at a party make the party more or less enjoyable for you or your partner?

You may agree that playing together is a good idea, but your ideas about what activities are fun may not match. One solution is to find a new activity to pursue together. Or, one partner may decide to develop an interest in an activity that the other enjoys.

Deciding how to have fun may cause problems. Taking turns making decisions is one approach. Another is to practice give-and-take, e.g. "I'll go to the Martins with you Friday if you will go to the basketball game with me Saturday."

A problem sometimes arises when one partner has a strong dislike for an activity that the other partner loves. The real issue often centers on the number of hours devoted to the activity. Some disagreements can be resolved by specifying the maximum number of hours per week each partner will devote to an activity that does not involve the other partner.

An Example of Recreation Conflict Solution

Wanting to surprise Judy, Phil made arrangements at a resort for the weekend. When he told Judy she seemed less than enthusiastic. She said she appreciated the thought but would have been just as happy to go to dinner and a movie. Phil was hurt that she was not excited about the plans.

Step 1. Mutual Respect. Phil needs to listen empathetically to Judy in order to convey respect for her reaction.

Phil: "Judy, I'm confused. I thought you would really be excited about this."

Judy: "I know you wanted to please me, and I appreciate that. I was just surprised that you didn't find out if I wanted to go. I feel a little resentful that you didn't let me in on the planning."

Step 2. Pinpoint the Real Issue. Through listening and reflecting, Phil can determine the underlying purpose of Judy's reaction. Her resentment is the clue that she feels upset because her right to decide was eliminated.

Phil: "Do you feel resentful because your feelings weren't considered?"

Judy: "I guess that is what's bothering me."

Step 3. Seek Areas of Agreement. In this example, the primary area of agreement Phil and Judy have reached is that they will talk about their feelings and will cooperate rather than bicker.

Step 4. Mutual Participation. Both Phil and Judy need to assume responsibility to resolve the problem. The process usually begins with one person making a proposal.

Judy: "I'd be willing to go away for the weekend with you if you would let me pick the place."

Phil: "I'm glad you want to go. It's fine with me if you want to choose as long as there's a swimming pool and tennis court."

Judy: "That's agreeable with me. How about the Whistling Pines?"

Phil: "Perfect!"

Use the conflict solution process to solve the following recreational challenge:

Al and Sally are opposites in many ways. Their differences for the most part complement one another, adding strength to their relationship. Their differences in what they enjoy doing for fun, however, present a major source of conflict. Al likes outdoor activities like fishing and hunting. Sally likes to be indoors, playing cards or bowling. What can they do?

Step 1._____

_____

Step 2._____

_____

Step 3._____

_____

Step 4._____

_____

The following questions may be helpful in determining if recreation is a problem in your marriage:

1. *How do we each prefer to spend our free time?*

2. *How much time should be spent in social activities? Personal activities? Active fun? Passive fun?*

3. *How much time should be spent together or alone on activities?*

4. *Do we need to consider some interests that we can pursue together?*

5. *Are we satisfied with what is happening in our lives during nonworking hours?*

6. *Does television watching absorb our free time? Do we need to make changes in this area?*

7. *Do we feel free to discuss issues related to how we spend our free time?*

8. *Does my partner have enough time and/or energy to share recreation with me?*

9. *Do we enjoy the same types of social events?*

10. *Am I concerned about the amount of time I spend with my partner? Do I feel I spend too little time? Too much time?*

The Challenge of Children

Of all the challenges that cause partners to seek professional help, one of the most common is the battle over how to handle their offspring. If partners have dissimilar values or come from different backgrounds, disputes may arise from genuine concern over what is really best for the child. Although it would be ideal, it is unrealistic to expect two people to always agree on how to raise their children. When partners disagree, they may decide to agree to disagree, which means it is okay to differ as long as you respect your partner's beliefs. It is important to support each other. Conflicting values not only cause problems between partners, but children are confused as well. Furthermore, it is harmful for children to sense that they have power to divide their mother and father.

It is unrealistic to expect two people to always agree on how to raise their children.

Conflicts over children usually can be resolved if the parents are aware of their own motivations and open to negotiation. The first question to ask is why a particular issue is so important to the parent. Partners must determine, for example, whether their practice of being strict and demanding or easygoing with the children relates more to their own priorities or to what is good for the children.

Although conflicts about how to rear children frequently develop, it is comforting to realize that parents are not supposed to agree on all aspects of child-rearing. It is important to have a procedure for settling differences when they occur so that the parents may deal with their children's behavior in an agreed-upon consistent manner. We recommend the approach found in *STEP Parent's Handbook* (Systematic Training for Effective Parenting)[3] and in *STEP/Teen*.[4] In addition, helpful information on parenting is found in *Raising a Responsible Child*[5] and in *The Basics of Adult/Teen Relationships*.[6]

An Example of Children Conflict Solution

Brady is Dixie and Roger's five-year-old son. Although Dixie and Roger are proud of Brady's quick wit and boundless energy, they are at odds over how to handle his unwillingness to put away his toys and pick up his room. Dixie thinks that if she doesn't force Brady to change, he'll pick up some bad habits. She is also tired of the extra work that he seems to purposely create. Roger feels that "boys will be boys" and that Brady is just going through a stage that will disappear if they don't make a big thing of it.

Step 1. Mutual Respect.

Dixie: "I can't stand his messes anymore. I feel as though my full-time job is picking things up after him."

Roger: "Are you angry because you have to pick up after Ronnie?"

Dixie: "Yes, and I'm also angry at you for not making him do it. You just don't seem to care."

Roger: "I know you'd like me to get after him more often, but I don't think that does any good. He'll get through this stage if you just ignore it."

Dixie: "Do you *really* think that if I ignore the mess he'll eventually pick up his room?"

Step 2. Pinpoint the Real Issue. Dixie seems really angry at Roger for not taking her concern more seriously. Roger doesn't condone Brady's behavior, but he doesn't respond emotionally to it like Dixie does.

Dixie: "I get really upset with you when you act this way. It seems as if only your way is right."

Roger: "Are you angry at me because I think I have the answer to the problem and you don't?"

Dixie: "Exactly. I think we're having a power contest over whose way of teaching Brady is right."

Step 3. Seek Areas of Agreement. Roger and Dixie now seem to be getting some insight into their real problems.

Roger: "I guess I haven't been willing to give an inch. And if we're going to find a solution, I'm going to have to be willing to change."

Dixie: "The way I'm handling Brady isn't doing any good either."

Step 4. Mutual Participation. Roger and Dixie have acknowledged that their respective parenting approaches are ineffective. They have assumed responsibility for trying a different approach.

Roger: "How about putting a box in the storage room, and whenever he leaves something lying around it gets put in the box for at least three days?"

Dixie: "I'm not sure he'll miss most of the stuff. But as soon as something that he really needs disappears, he'll see the light. It'll get his junk out of the way—one way or another."

Roger: "Are you willing to do this for two weeks?"

Dixie: "I am willing if you promise to do it, too."

Roger: "I will."

Use the conflict solution process to develop a solution for the following challenge concerning children:

Both Juan and Fran love their children and are willing to sacrifice for them. They have a problem in involving the children in work around the house. Fran believes that children should be allowed to do as much or little as they decide. Juan, on the other hand, wants to assign chores to the children each week. The children are receiving confusing messages and, not surprisingly, are avoiding working around the house. The issue has become the focal point of unhappiness in their home, and the parents have several violent arguments about the issue every week.

Step 1._____

_____

Step 2._____

_____

Step 3._____

_____

Step 4._____

_____

The Challenge of In-laws

In-laws provide a nearly universal and potentially dangerous threat to marital happiness. Trouble with in-laws usually begins early in marriage and sometimes is resolved only when parents die. Even then, the trouble can leave a residual of discontent hindering an otherwise happy marital relationship. Some parents have a hard time letting go of their children, and they consequently interfere in the lives of their married children.

It is the responsibility of the married son or daughter to set the limits of parental involvement. The needs of a partner should always take precedence over the needs of a parent if marital harmony is to be maintained. It is almost impossible for an in-law problem to get out of hand when husband and wife value each other's happiness more than the happiness of their parents. Although parents should always be important to us, they cannot be the first priority in a healthy marriage.

IT'S OKAY, MOM...
CALL ANYTIME.
HAROLD UNDERSTANDS.

Although parents should always be important
to us, they cannot be the first priority in
a healthy marriage.

Few partners can criticize their in-laws without risking criticism of their own parents in return. Neither partner should be put in the position of having to defend a parent's behavior. We didn't pick our parents. They were given to us. We cannot answer for their behavior but only for our own. That goes for brothers and sisters, as well as aunts and uncles, all who potentially are part of in-law problems. It is inappropriate for you to have to defend your parents or family members to your partner. Parents and relatives are people, and some people are healthier than others. You cannot change your parents' behavior, but you do have the capacity to change your own behavior.

An Example of In-Law Conflict Solution

After Scott and Joyce were married they moved into a small apartment in the basement of Scott's parents' home in order to save money. Because Scott's mother wanted to help the newlyweds she would cook meals, make special desserts, do laundry, and purchase tickets for movies and plays—to attend with the parents, of course. Joyce began to feel as though she were Scott's sister and not his wife. Joyce wanted to run her own house and life, but she didn't want to upset Scott or her in-laws.

Step 1. Mutual Respect. It is important to take risks in conflict resolution. When couples have an agreement to mutually respect each other's viewpoint, the risk is lessened.

Scott: "Don't you like doing things with my parents?"

Joyce: "I do like your parents, but it seems that we do everything with them."

Scott: "You would like to do things without them around?"

Joyce: "I wouldn't mind doing *some* things with them, but I want us to have a life of our own."

Step 2. Pinpoint the Real Issue. One partner often feels like an outsider when activities center around relatives. Joyce married Scott and agreed to spend her life with him, not his parents.

Scott: "I haven't been very sensitive to your needs. I thought that by letting my parents do so many things for us it would make things easier for you. Now I can see that I didn't consider your feelings."

Joyce: "I do appreciate all that your parents have done. I just feel powerless in my own home and would like to make some decisions about our life."

Scott: "I can see that I haven't had to change my life at all. I guess I need to grow up and break the ties with mom and dad."

Step 3. Seek Areas of Agreement. Joyce and Scott now realize how they have let their well-meaning "mom" disrupt their marriage. Receiving help made life easier in surface ways but created other problems at the same time. It is encouraging that both Joyce and Scott agree that a change needs to take place.

Joyce: "I'm glad you understand how difficult this is for me and agree that we need to make some changes."

Scott "If we don't do it now, it'll only get worse."

Step 4. Mutual Participation. Clearly identifying the problem paves the way for effective conflict solution in which both partners participate.

Scott: "I don't know what we can do. If we break away totally my parents might be hurt."

Joyce: "I'm not asking for a complete break with them. How about if we agree to have two meals with them each week and go out with them no more than once a week?"

Scott: "Maybe we need to make the break a little more slowly so it doesn't seem like something is really wrong. How about if we have two dinners during the week and one on the weekend to start?"

Joyce: "That sounds good."

Use the conflict solution process to solve the following in-law challenge:

Keith and Cindy have been married for a short time. Keith is at the end of his rope with his father-in-law. Cindy's father calls or visits every weekend. He tells Keith how to plan a budget, he points out things that need repairing in the house, and he tells Keith when he thinks the lawn needs mowing. Even though Keith thinks that his father-in-law means well, he still feels put down by all the advice and criticism.

Step 1._____

_____

Step 2._____

_____

Step 3._____

_____

Step 4._____

_____

The following questions may help in determining if in-laws are a problem in your marriage:

1. *What are your relatives' attitudes toward your marriage?*

2. *What do you perceive as differences in values between your two families?*

3. *Are you comfortable in the presence of each other's families?*

4. *Do you think your partner is too involved with his or her family? Does your partner think you are too involved with your family?*

The Challenge of Religion

Most of what we initially learn about what is right and what is wrong comes from our family upbringing. Frequently these values are related to a specific religious background. Religious beliefs and practices contribute positively to a marriage when they are acceptable to both partners. Problems begin when one partner's religious practices conflict with the other partner's. To help you explore the influence of religious upbringing on your marriage, use these questions written by Ann G. Ruben as a basis for discussion:

• *Were your parents atheists? Agnostics? Were they affiliated with a particular religious group? Were you included?*

• *Did your parents have definite attitudes toward people of different religious beliefs? How did your parents express their attitudes?*

• *Did they use religion to control your behavior? Did they use religion to give you a sense of appreciation and wonder of life? To give comfort and security? To explain natural phenomena?*

- *What did they say about religious beliefs? Did they agree with each other?*
- *How did they practice their beliefs? Were what they said and did consistent?[7]*

Different faiths put different demands on their followers. Each of us interprets these demands from our own perspective. In a marriage in which each partner has an intense commitment to a different religion, the couple may agree to disagree and leave it at that. This means they do not have to agree with their partner's position, but they respect the partner's religious practices. Some couples choose to attend a church that represents a compromise between the beliefs of their former churches. Others alternate attending each other's church. Some couples work things out by one partner's following the wishes of the partner who seems more devout.

When children are involved, the couples have four options. They may decide to teach their children the religions of both parents. They may agree that the children be reared in the faith of the more devout parent. They may resolve to give the children no religious instruction. Or, their children may receive instruction in a church that both find acceptable.

An Example of Resolution of a Religious Conflict

Marilyn and Ted have been happily married for seven years. They share many of the same interests and have been able to work out most of their conflicts. Ted was raised in the Jewish faith and Marilyn was raised a devout Catholic. Neither Ted nor Marilyn shows great tolerance of the other's beliefs. They did not consider this a big problem in their relationship because everything else was so right. Recently, however, they have had conflict over how to spend holidays and observe religious celebrations. A new, larger issue has surfaced. Marilyn is now pregnant, and they are having frequent arguments about the religious training the child will have.

Step 1. Mutual Respect. Before effective conflict resolution can occur, both partners must feel that their point of view is understood and respected.

Ted:	"I don't want my child growing up with beliefs that are different from mine."
Marilyn:	"Your religion is important to you, and you want your children to share it with you. I understand that perfectly because I feel the same way."
Ted:	"I guess I'm being selfish, Marilyn, but that's how I feel."

Step 2. Pinpoint the Real Issue. Even though this may be an emotion-laden situation, effective listening can help uncover the underlying purpose of the conflict.

Marilyn:	"Could it be that we both believe that our religious beliefs are superior?"
Ted:	"Or, maybe neither of us wants to admit that there is truth in a religion other than our own. Neither of us really wants to change."
Marilyn:	"That sure seems to be the case."

Step 3. Seek Areas of Agreement. Marilyn and Ted need to identify what agreements they have. The fact that they have so much in common other than religion and that they agree that a religious education is important for their child are beginners.

Ted:	"It's clear that we both want our child to have a religious education."
Marilyn:	"But how can a person follow two religions?"

Step 4. Mutual Participation. Both Ted and Marilyn need to assume responsibility to resolve the problem. The process begins with one person making a proposal.

Marilyn:	"The child could learn about both religions by going to both churches. We could alternate weeks taking the child to our own church."
Ted:	"That would work out all right for weekly worship, but what about special services?"
Marilyn:	"How about taking turns whenever a conflict occurs?"
Ted:	"I can live with that agreement."

Use the conflict solution process to develop a solution to the following religious challenge:

Paul and Mary belong to a church. Mary is very involved in church activities. However, Paul attends only now and then. Early in their marriage Mary accepted Paul's level of church involvement. However, now that their children are old enough for religious education, Mary feels that it is Paul's duty to become more active in the church. She frequently tells Paul that she's disappointed that he doesn't get more involved. Paul sees no need for his church involvement to change. How can Mary and Paul resolve this conflict?

Step 1._____

_____

Step 2._____

_____

Step 3._____

_____

Step 4._____

_____

The following questions may help in determining if religion is a problem in your marriage:

1. *Is it hard for you to accept some of the practices of your religion? Of your partner's religion?*

2. *Are you dissatisfied with your religious practices? Personally? As a couple?*

3. *Does religion mean the same to you as it does to your partner?*

4. *Is church attendance important for you? Your children?*

5. *Do you and your partner agree on how to put your religious beliefs into practice?*

6. *Is it important for you to pray with your partner?*

The Challenge of Friends

Social contact with friends supplements a healthy marriage, enriching the marital atmosphere and cushioning it against the inevitable difficulties and conflicts of married life. Marriage that is part of a larger unit, including friends, gains stability and security.

Friends can provide a rewarding, enriching extension to a couple's life.

Good mutual friends add to the happiness of any marriage. Problems sometimes surface in marriages when partners have friends that are not mutual friends. Partners should feel free to pursue friendships with different people. Often, the real issue concerns the amount of time a partner spends with friends, rather than the fact that the partners have different friends. Or, a partner insists that "my friends should be your friends, too."

A potentially larger problem for a couple is to have no friends. Ours is a mobile society. We move often, leaving good friends behind. Or when good friends move, we are left behind. Vance Packard calls us "a nation of strangers."[8] When a couple experiences such change, it is important to find ways to make new friends. Friends provide a rewarding, enriching extension to a couple's life.

An Example of a Friendship Conflict Solution

Kay and Sara have been best friends since childhood. Since Sara married Chuck, there has been little time for her to spend with Kay. Sara resents this and would like to have more time to spend with Kay. Chuck feels that he doesn't get enough of Sara's time now. He would like to see her spend even less time with Kay. This has resulted in frequent shouting matches and no apparent solution.

Step 1. Mutual Respect. It is important to be empathic whenever hurt feelings are present.

Sara: "I resent not being able to spend more time with Kay. Whenever I bring up the topic, you seem to become so weird."

Chuck: "You're angry with me because I don't like you spending time with Kay!"

Sara: "Yes. You seem jealous of her."

Chuck: "Maybe I am. I don't get to spend enough time with you, and I may even get less of your time because of Kay."

Sara: "I didn't realize that you feel we don't spend enough time together."

Step 2. Pinpoint the Real Issue. It is important to keep the dialogue going by agreeing to allow each other to make guesses about what is really going on.

Chuck: "I get the feeling that you want to be able to run your own life and do things just to show me you can."

Sara: "My father controlled my mom, and I won't let that happen to me."

Chuck: "I guess I sensed that. Whenever you seem to be trying to prove something, I feel hurt and want to get even with you."

Step 3. Seek Areas of Agreement. Sara and Chuck are willing to accept their roles in the problem.

Sara: "I can see how I upset you."

Chuck: "And I took the bait and acted like a child."

Step 4. Mutual Participation.

Chuck: "Why don't you and Kay set aside a regular day to get together each week? If I know what day you'll be busy, I'll see if I can get Jim or Bob to play golf or racquet ball."

Sara: "I like the idea of getting together each week, but I don't want to be tied down to the same day."

Chuck: "I don't care what day it is as long as I have enough time to make other plans."

Sara: "How about if I try to give you two days' notice?"

Chuck: "That sounds fair."

Use the conflict solution process to develop a solution to the following friendship challenge:

Both Dale and Brigit work outside the home. Dale looks forward to the weekend as a time to relax and spend quiet time with his family. Brigit, on the other hand, sees the weekend as a chance to get out and visit with friends or to plan other social activities. Both are disappointed with their time together because it seems as if one is always forcing the other to do what he or she wants.

Step 1._____

_____

Step 2._____

_____

Step 3._____

_____

Step 4._____

_____

The following questions may be helpful in determining if friends are a problem in your marriage:

1. *Do you like your partner's friends? Does your partner like your friends?*
2. *Are you uncomfortable when your partner spends time with friends?*
3. *Are you uncomfortable when your partner spends time with friends of the other sex?*
4. *Are you comfortable with the amount of time your partner spends with friends?*

Challenge of Alcohol and Drugs

There are an estimated ten million alcoholics in the United States alone. In the past the majority of alcoholics were men, but the number of women alcoholics is sharply increasing. A person may be considered an alcoholic or a problem drinker if alcohol interferes with his or her economic, social, or physical well-being. When drinking impedes one's ability to get or keep a job or when it disrupts interpersonal relationships, it is a problem! Some of the consequences of problem drinking include weight change, headaches, agitation, confusion, hallucinations, gastrointestinal inflammation, and liver disorders.[9]

A marriage that includes a compulsive drinker or drug abuser is in serious need of professional help. The lives of both partners, and often the children as well, are dominated by the problem. The family lives in a world of lies, fear, denial, shame, and guilt.

Alcoholism and drug abuse can be treated. Rarely can either problem be treated by a partner or marriage counselor alone. People endure humiliation and even physical abuse in an attempt to help a partner break an addictive habit. Such efforts are usually futile and frustrating. Partners of alcoholics must understand the motivation of the alcoholic, their own role in relation to the problem, and their options.

Alcoholism usually stems from a lack of self-esteem. Alcoholics are discouraged people. Various factors can be involved including guilt, inadequacy, helplessness, and the inability to cope with life. The most critical factor, however, is the negative sense of self. With such disastrously low self-esteem comes the need to escape. Alcohol blots out a reality that seems too overwhelming to face.

Denial is an important part of the alcoholic's escape. When confronted, the alcoholic continues to deny the problem, and the partner typically accepts the denial. We do not want to believe our partner is lying to us or has a serious problem. When both partners recognize and accept alcoholism as a problem, recovery begins. But acknowledging the problem is painful and often unbearable to the alcoholic who already suffers from fragile self-esteem.

Understanding the alcoholic's need for denial can lessen frustration and resentment about the constant lies. If the partner realizes that the problem stems from within the alcoholic, there usually is less guilt. Recognizing what a self-destructive pattern alcoholism is may give a partner the strength to risk the alcoholic's anger, overcome the denial, and say in a loving way, "You need help that I can't give you. I wish I could, but I don't know what to do. You have a drinking problem and you *must* get professional help. I'm more than willing to give you every kind of support that I can, but I won't stand by any longer and watch you destroy yourself. I won't continue living with you in this way." In a marriage in which the partner refuses to get help, the other partner can go alone to a family support group, such as AlAnon, to receive specific and concrete help.

There are always at least two people involved when there is alcoholism in a marriage. One partner unconsciously helps the other to remain alcoholic. The collusion is neither deliberate nor malicious. Believing they are helping, non-alcoholic partners unwittingly feed into the pattern of the addict. Either scorn or pity may be just what is needed to perpetuate feelings that lead the alcoholic to drink. The non-alcoholic partner contributes to the problem by continuing to tolerate, live with, aid, or support the alcoholic.

The unconscious reason for the collusion may be that the partner is unwilling to consider separation because he or she is afraid to lose the security of marriage. Fear of facing the alcoholic's rage or self-destruction also keeps people from taking action. There is really little hope for improvement without help such as that recommended by professionals such as Alcoholics Anonymous and AlAnon.[10]

An Example of an Alcohol Conflict Solution

Vernon is public relations director for a large corporation. Many of the meetings and dinners he attends involve social drinking. Margaret has noticed for some time that Vernon always comes home with alcohol on his breath, and he heads for the liquor cabinet as soon as he arrives. She likes to have a cocktail with him and talk over his day, but she is worried about his drinking and doesn't want to support it.

Step 1. Mutual Respect. Vernon needs to listen empathetically without reacting until he is sure he understands what Margaret is communicating. This will facilitate mutual respect and increase the probability of successful resolution.

Margaret: "I'm really worried about how much you're drinking. Even though I enjoy a cocktail with you after work, I don't want you to think that your drinking is okay with me."

Vernon: "You're concerned that I'm drinking too much?"

Margaret: "I'm worried that you may be becoming addicted, and I'm confused about how to help you stop."

Vernon: "I know I drink too much, but I don't know why."

Step 2. Pinpoint the Real Issue. Margaret realizes that Vernon uses lack of understanding as an excuse for not taking responsibility for the problem.

Margaret: "I get really upset when I hear you tell me you don't know why you drink. I feel you use that as an excuse for not changing."

Vernon: "Maybe you're right. By acting as if I don't understand, I don't have to try to change."

Margaret: "I never should have let you hide behind your excuse."

Step 3. Seek Areas of Agreement. Vernon and Margaret have been making good progress. They still need to cooperate in solving their problem.

Margaret: "I'm relieved that at last we both are admitting that we're aware that you're drinking too much. Now maybe we can choose to do something about it."

Vernon: "I know I've got to do something."

Margaret: "And I'm not going to sit back and let you drink so much without a loud protest."

Step 4. Mutual Participation. With a problem as complicated as alcoholism, it is frequently necessary to work toward agreeing to get outside help.

Margaret: "Will you get some professional help? I think you should go to an A.A. meeting."

Vernon: "I'm really not convinced that the problem's that serious. But I guess A.A. will help me find out."

Use the conflict solution process to develop a solution to the following alcohol challenge:

Frank and Janella got married shortly after college graduation. They continued living in a college town, and much of their social life revolved around a campus bar. Frank has become increasingly aware that a day rarely goes by that Janella doesn't have four or five drinks. He also notices that all of their social events center around drinking. When he confronted Janella with his observation, she told him, "Get off my back."

Step 1._____

_____

Step 2._____

_____

Step 3._____

_____

Step 4._____

_____

The following questions may help determine if alcohol is a problem in your marriage:

1. *Do you feel that your partner drinks too much?*
2. *Do you feel that you drink too much?*
3. *What percentage of your social activities involve some form of alcohol?*
4. *Can you talk about alcohol and drug abuse without one partner becoming angry?*

Other Challenges

Potential sources of conflict are unlimited. What may seem inconsequential to one couple may be an explosive issue to another couple. Problems can arise over virtually any issue that surfaces in a couple's life together, issues as varied as housework; driving the car; one partner's moodiness, or violent behavior, or depression; lack of comfort; dual careers; lateness; and maintaining physical attractiveness. When a couple recognizes that conflict is inevitable and learns to redefine conflict as *challenge*, any issue can be resolved given time, effort, and patience. There is always more than one solution to any marriage challenge. Each couple needs to work out their own agreements and solutions. They may not welcome conflict with open arms, but they can develop confidence in their ability to manage conflict, and they can grow in the process.

References

1. William H. Masters and Virginia E. Johnson, *Human Sexual Response*, (Boston: Little, Brown & Co., 1974).
2. Hugh Prather, *A Book of Games*, (Garden City, NY: Doubleday, 1981), p. 70.
3. Don Dinkmeyer and Gary D. McKay, *Systematic Training for Effective Parenting: Parent's Handbook*, (Circle Pines, MN: American Guidance Service, 1976).
4. Don Dinkmeyer and Gary D. McKay, *STEP/Teen*, (Circle Pines, MN: American Guidance Service, 1983).
5. Don Dinkmeyer and Gary D. McKay, *Raising a Responsible Child*, (NY: Simon and Schuster, 1973).
6. Don Dinkmeyer, *The Basics of Adult/Teen Relationships*, (CMTI Press, Box 8268, Coral Springs, FL 33075, 1976).
7. Ann G. Ruben, *Creating a Mature Marriage*, (CAMM Programs, P.O. Box 640358, Miami, FL 33164, 1980), pp. 85-86.
8. Vance Packard, *Nation of Strangers*, (NY: David McKay Co., 1972).
9. David Knox, *Dr. Knox's Marital Exercise Book*, (NY: David McKay Co., 1975).
10. Laura J. Singer, *Stages: The Crises that Shape Your Marriage*, (NY: Grosset & Dunlap, 1980).

Questions

1. What is meant by the statement, "There is no 'normal' sexual relationship?"
2. Why are communication skills so important in a couple's sexual relationship?
3. Do you feel it's important that both partners be involved in financial planning and budgeting? Why or why not?
4. How can spending recreation time together help a relationship?
5. Do partners need to have the same parenting style? What may happen if they don't?
6. The authors state that a parent's needs should not take priority over a partner's needs? Do you agree?
7. What role do good friends play in marital happiness?
8. "There are always two people involved when there is alcoholism in a marriage." Do you agree with this statement? Why or why not?

Activity for the Week

Continue Daily Dialogue, and hold Encouragement Meetings and a Marriage Meeting.

As a couple, develop goals and plans for the next six months in your marriage. Be specific. Write them down.

To help you assess your goals and progress, fill in MY PLAN.

Fill in the Marital Self-evaluation found at the end of Chapter 9.

1. A good sexual relationship requires the highest degree of communication.

2. Financial problems often appear to be the grounds for collapse of a marriage. However, deeper reasons, such as an overemphasis on personal prestige or superiority, commonly emerge as the real issue.

3. Happy, meaningful relationships depend on setting aside time for regular play. Finding ways to have fun together is a challenge couples often overlook.

4. Parents can resolve child-rearing conflicts if they become aware of their own motivations and are willing to negotiate.

5. The needs of a partner should always take precedence over the needs of parents and other relatives if marital harmony is to be maintained.

6. When partners differ in their religious beliefs or practices they may reach an acceptable compromise, or they may agree to disagree.

7. Close friends can add to the happiness of a marriage, but difficulties may arise if the partners disagree on the amount of time available to spend with friends. A potentially larger problem is for a couple to have no friends.

8. When one partner has a problem with alcoholism, both partners are involved. The non-alcoholic partner contributes to the problem by continuing to tolerate, live with, aid, or support the alcoholic.

MY ◆ PLAN

Ways I can encourage _____
_____

Strengths I can use to improve the relationship _____
_____

Ways I can show I care or appreciate _____
_____

Ways I can improve my communication _____
_____

Effective ways I can resolve conflict _____
_____

I am ready and willing to change my behavior in the following way(s): _____
_____

MY PROGRESS IN APPLYING THESE SKILLS	I am doing this more	I need to do this more	I remain about the same
Listening to feelings			
Communicating honestly			
Encouraging			
Daily dialogue			
Communicating love			
Encouragement meetings			
Marriage meetings			
Resolving conflict effectively			
Demonstrating specific caring behavior			
Choosing a better marriage			
Spending time with my partner			

MARITAL SELF-EVALUATION

Circle the number that reflects how you feel about each item below at this time:

POSITIVE

NEGATIVE

10	9	8	7	6		5	4	3	2	1

1. I understand my goals and my partner's goals. / I do not understand my goals and my partner's goals.

10	9	8	7	6		5	4	3	2	1

2. I encourage my partner. / I don't encourage my partner.

10	9	8	7	6		5	4	3	2	1

3. I listen to my partner. / I don't listen to my partner.

10	9	8	7	6		5	4	3	2	1

4. I recognize and understand my partner's feelings. / I don't recognize and understand my partner's feelings.

10	9	8	7	6		5	4	3	2	1

5. I can see the positive potential in situations. / I am pessimistic.

10	9	8	7	6		5	4	3	2	1

6. My communication with my partner is honest and open. / My communication is not open and honest.

10	9	8	7	6		5	4	3	2	1

7. I believe I am responsible for my own positive self-esteem. / I blame my partner and others for my lack of self-esteem.

10	9	8	7	6		5	4	3	2	1

8. I plan and communicate my intentions openly. / I fail to plan and communicate my intentions.

10	9	8	7	6		5	4	3	2	1

9. I recognize and choose my behavior and beliefs. / I am a victim of my behavior and beliefs.

10	9	8	7	6		5	4	3	2	1

10. I resolve conflict with my partner. / I try to get my way or prove I am right.

10	9	8	7	6		5	4	3	2	1

11. I spend enough quality time with my partner. / I spend little quality time with my partner.

10	9	8	7	6		5	4	3	2	1

12. We share marriage responsibilities in a fair manner. / We do not share marriage responsibilities.

10	9	8	7	6		5	4	3	2	1

13. We have fun in many different ways. / We do not know how to have fun.

Circle the number that represents your current level of satisfaction in each of the following areas:

1 = dissatisfied   5 = average satisfaction   10 = very satisfied

14. Work	1	2	3	4	5	6	7	8	9	10
15. Management of household chores	1	2	3	4	5	6	7	8	9	10
16. Social interaction with each other	1	2	3	4	5	6	7	8	9	10
17. Social interaction with other people	1	2	3	4	5	6	7	8	9	10
18. Demonstration of affection	1	2	3	4	5	6	7	8	9	10
19. Sexual relationship	1	2	3	4	5	6	7	8	9	10
20. Meaning of life and spirituality	1	2	3	4	5	6	7	8	9	10
21. Parenting	1	2	3	4	5	6	7	8	9	10
22. Leisure and recreation	1	2	3	4	5	6	7	8	9	10
23. Family finances	1	2	3	4	5	6	7	8	9	10
24. Time together (Quantity and quality)	1	2	3	4	5	6	7	8	9	10

In an equal marriage, there is no artificial division of labor.

Self~help Procedures for Maintaining Your Marriage

I sometimes wish I had been born a hundred years ago," the young man said. "It must have been simpler to be married then!" When today's couples grapple with complicated schedules, dual careers, and "unlimited opportunities" to do more and be more, it is understandable that they would sometimes yearn for what seems to have been a simpler time—a time when the priorities and expectations for marriage were clear. The man was expected to provide a home, food, and the basic necessities. The woman was expected to bear children, take care of the household, and prepare the meals.

The man who would really have liked more time at home or the relief of having another wage earner in the family would have had a difficult time discussing his wishes with his friends. The woman who wanted to help run the family business or get a college education had to content herself with the pleasure of seeing the row of pickle jars she had just filled.

The priorities and expectations for our marriages are indeed different than they were a hundred years ago. And in your marriage they may be different than they were a year ago or should be a year from now. If we are to maintain a satisfying marriage, we need to establish guidelines for our marriage now and a process to deal with inevitable changes in the future.

Equal Marriage

Because we create our relationships, we have the power to change patterns of relating that are no longer meaningful. Learning to live as equals in marriage allows us not only to attain greater personal fulfillment but also to develop a more effective marriage relationship.

The concept of equal marriage is widely misunderstood, primarily because of attempts to define equality solely in terms of division of labor. Equal marriage does *not* mean an absolute 50-50 split of the work. In an equal marriage partners have equal rights to develop as persons and equal responsibilities for taking care of themselves, each other, and their children. Each partner bears equal responsibility for the success and survival of the relationship. In an equal marriage there is not an artificial division of labor according to sex roles. Decisions about who will be responsible for what are made after taking into consideration the wants, needs, skills, likes, and dislikes of each partner. Important decisions either are made together or, by agreement, are designated to one or the other partner, keeping in mind abilities and interests.

Equal partners may influence each other by compliments, critiques, and suggestions, but the final decision in more private matters rests with each individual. How to decorate an office, how to spend small amounts of money, how to dress, or how to think are not matters to be dictated by a partner.

When partners free themselves from traditional role expectations that impose an artificial separation of tasks, goals, and emotions, companionship and intimacy increase. Many couples are reluctant to give up the security of traditional roles. However, roles partners assume from custom rather than from mutual decisions provide false security.

Our psychological and biological needs influence our ability to live together as equals in a marriage relationship. Clifford Sager and Bernice Hunt developed a list of questions to help individuals become aware of how their inner needs influence marital expectations.[1] The following checklist, adapted from Sager and Hunt's material, will help you assess how personality characteristics currently contribute to or detract from equality in your marriage relationship. Take time to consider each item in the checklist as it relates to your perception of your partner. Share your perceptions with each other. How do you feel about your partner's perceptions of your behavior?

Ideally, you will each have the majority of items checked in the *yes* column. Items checked *no* may provide a basis for discussion. Make time for discussion in one of your marriage meetings.

What Do We Want from Our Marriage?

All couples have expectations that marriage will meet certain needs and desires, and assumptions of how the marriage *should* function. These expectations and assumptions form an implicit contract. However, partners rarely make their contract explicit by deciding and planning together how to meet these needs and desires or how to resolve conflict when desires and needs are not met.

Change is inevitable. Conflict is inevitable. Implicit contracts are poor guides when conflict occurs. Whose rules have we broken? Why am I happy and you're not happy? Why do the rules apply to me and not to you?

A couple may live together in relative comfort by avoiding challenging issues in their marriage. A truly satisfying marriage, however, requires a willingness to deal with challenges as they occur. A couple needs to ask themselves: Have we identified the strong and weak areas in our marriage? What strategies can we agree to use to build on the strengths and improve the weaknesses?

Some couples grapple constantly with major issues and never solve day-to-day conflicts. Others bicker over everyday irritations and never glimpse the larger issues. Healthy marriages need a way of dealing with both challenges. We do need to know where we agree and disagree in areas that are common challenges in marriage. And we need a method for bringing about specific changes on a day-to-day basis, a method that allows us to build on strengths at the same time we improve weaknesses. We build an explicit contract for our marriage by identifying what we want and deciding on a method to help us achieve what we want.

Checklist of Equal Partner Behavior

Yes	No	
———	———	1. Tends to be independent. Is also cooperative and interdependent.
———	———	2. Is active and assertive.
———	———	3. Is capable of close, sustained intensity without clinging.
———	———	4. Is able to show strength by sharing or assuming responsibility for making decisions and allows me to do the same. Is neither submissive nor domineering.
———	———	5. Has no great fear of losing partner.
———	———	6. Does not seek to control me or to be controlled by me.
———	———	7. Has low to moderate level of anxiety.
———	———	8. Sexual responsiveness ranges from moderate to high.
———	———	9. Has excellent capacity to love self and mate.
———	———	10. Has a well-developed and well-defined style of problem solving but also respects my style.

Healthy marriages deal with day-to-day conflicts as well as larger issues.

The following questions will help you assess your relationship in areas that are common challenges to marriage.

Financial Matters Do you have a realistic budget? Can each of you have your own financial assets or personal property? How much money can you spend without consulting your partner? Who has the responsibility for finances? How much money do you feel you should save each month? What are you saving for? What place does money have in your relationship? Is it understood as power? Love? Who controls the money?

Recreation Do you enjoy time together and time apart? What are your common interests? Does either of you insist that the other participate in an activity that only one of you enjoys? Do you feel anxious or guilty if you don't always join forces? Do you respect or resent differences in leisure-related interests? How many evenings out each week do you want to spend as a couple? How many evenings alone? At home with friends? Who plans the events? Who arranges for child care?

Children Do you agree on the number of children you want? If there are children, do you agree on child-rearing responsibilities? Who has more authority with the children? Do you compete with your partner for their love?

Family and Friends Do you have a good relationship with friends, parents, and in-laws? Does either of you resent the other's family? Do you resent the way your partner relates to his or her family? Do you support your partner in issues discussed with parents or relatives? How do you feel about each other's friends? What do you want from friendships?

Religious Orientation Do you agree on religious values and beliefs? Where differences exist, can you resolve your differences so that both of you can follow your beliefs?

Sharing Responsibility What responsibilities do you expect each of you to assume? Who does the housework, cooking, and shopping? Who takes major responsibility for earning income? For child care? For planning vacations? For planning entertainment? Who makes decisions? Does one partner control the relationship? In what areas?

Marital Cohesion How close do you feel to your partner? Are you satisfied with the amount of time you spend together? How much dependence or independence should each partner have? What do you need permission for? How much possession and control of each other do you want in your relationship? How much time per day or per week can each partner have privacy?

Marital Adaptability Are you and your partner flexible? Should the marriage relationship take priority over all other interests (for example, work, children, friends)? How much closeness and intimacy do you want? What should a partner do if he or she feels a need for more independence? What are your short- and long-range career plans? Plans for children?

Marital Satisfaction Are you satisfied with most aspects of your marriage? In what areas do you feel let down by your mate? What in your relationship could cause trouble? Does one of you owe the other anything for making a considerable sacrifice (such as putting the other through school, quitting a career to stay home to raise a family)? What would be considered a fair return?

Communication Do you feel your partner understands you? Are you able to share your feelings? How open is your communication? Can you clearly express all of your feelings? Are you each responsible for your own feelings, needs, and attitudes? Is it agreed that while each influences the other, neither of you is responsible for keeping the other happy? Do you agree to give support, comfort, and nurture when one partner needs and asks for such? How should you handle an unhealthy dependency?

Personality Do you like the personality and habits of your partner? Are your life styles different? Is one partner outgoing and the other a loner? How do you feel about yourself as a man or woman? Does your partner still interest you? Do you have different energy levels?

Conflict Do you feel that you are able to discuss and resolve differences with your partner? How do you approach problems? Do you bring your problems and resentments to your partner as soon as you realize you have them? Should you or your partner wait to discuss issues until the problems are better understood? Do you have ground rules for resolving arguments? If your differences become overwhelming, will you call a third-party negotiator? Who should you call? A professional counselor? A friend? A minister?

Sexual Relationship Do you feel comfortable discussing sexual issues and preferences? Is sex approached enthusiastically or as a duty?

When you have answered the questions note the issues that you want to discuss. Marriage meetings provide an opportunity to take the necessary time to work toward agreement in these crucial areas. **Use the following communication skills as you discuss.**

1. *Work on one issue, disagreement, or misunderstanding at a time.* Do not try to resolve all the problems in one sitting or over a short period of time. Remember, it took time for these issues to develop to a point of misunderstanding or disagreement, and it will take time to resolve them.

2. *When you talk remember that you are evaluating the relationship.* Do not analyze the other person. You can only change yourself. Even without cooperation a relationship can improve when one person begins to change. One partner's growth and change often pro-

vides motivation for the other partner to change.

3. *Remember that the opinions, values, and needs of each of you are valid and important.* There is no right or wrong position. Your partner's behavior is an honest expression of self.

4. *Discuss issues and problems in a way that does not threaten your partner.* Phrase your concerns in ways that reflect your own feelings rather than in ways that blame. Listen to the other person. Really listen. You may find that you have been taking things for granted that just aren't true. You may find that you do and say things that are destructive to the other person's feelings of self-worth and integrity.

Sometimes our communication diverts attention from the real issue.

5. *Assert yourself quietly and to the point when something is really important.* Self-assertion differs from aggression. You can assert yourself by calmly stating how you *feel*, what you *think*, and what you *will do* (rather than what you refuse to do). "I am upset when I get stuck with all the house cleaning. I plan to call the cleaning service if this happens again."

6. *Work out a method for making decisions that does not place all responsibility for the decision and its results on one person.* All of those who will be affected by the decision should participate. This is particularly true when decisions affect children. Children need to be respected as individuals and should be allowed to participate in making family decisions even though they do not determine the direction a family takes. Children's views of a particular issue often lend valuable insight and information that you may have overlooked. A decision has a greater probability of bringing successful action when the people involved have all participated in the decision.

7. *Work at becoming a better communicator.* Communication is a dynamic process. It involves more than words. Learn to discern the difference between true communication and communication that is designed to divert attention from the real issue. Notice the nonverbal communication of the other person. Develop an understanding and awareness of your impact upon other people. Are you communicating what you *think* you are communicating?

8. *Repeat the statement of the other person to be sure you understand.* If a person says, "You think you know everything. You never listen to me," you respond by saying, "You mean you think I believe I'm always right and that I don't really listen to your opinions?"

The above method can be an invaluable aid in discovering areas of unresolved conflict in your relationship. Remember that acceptance of the accuracy of the other person's viewpoint and honest, open discussion are essential in dealing with these complex issues.

What is Right With Our Marriage?

It is important to recognize and continue actions that currently please you and your partner. Many of the things that make marriages work go unnoticed. In time they may disappear unless they are nourished through encouragement.

• List eight things that your partner does that you like. Be as specific as possible.

• Choose four that are the most important. Make sure each item is expressed in concrete terms, referring to something that your partner *does* rather than *is*.

• Indicate how many times it was done during the last seven days. Indicate how many times you would like to see it done during the next week.

• Share your list with your partner. Be sure you both are clear about each item on your respective lists.

• When both partners are sure they understand each other's lists, select items from each list that you each agree to do during the next week. Post the final agreement.

• Evaluate and renegotiate at a follow-up meeting in one week.

This form is helpful for recording a specific agreement.

Pleasing List

Week of _____

1. I agree to continue _____

_____

at least _____ times this week.
2. I agree to continue _____

_____

at least _____ times this week.
3. I agree to continue _____

_____

at least _____ times this week.
4. I agree to continue _____

_____

at least _____ times this week.

Signature _____

Next Meeting _____
                        date   time

Making Specific Changes

What specific changes do you want to see in your marriage? In other words, what specific things does your partner do or not do that you feel need to be changed?

- Write out the changes you would like your partner to make. List these changes as specific behaviors such as "Come home Fridays by 5:30 p.m., or call" rather than, "Be more thoughtful."
- Describe a series of actions that can actually be accomplished during the week that will bring about the desired change.
- Choose the four changes that are most important to you. Be sure each item is in concrete terms, referring to something your partner can *do* rather than something your partner *is*. For example, "I want you to put the toothpaste away when you are finished" rather than "I wish you wouldn't be so messy."
- Share your list with your partner. Be sure you both understand the items listed.
- When both partners clearly understand the lists, begin to negotiate an agreement. Post the final agreement and schedule a follow-up meeting for the next week.
- During the follow-up meeting, evaluate the past week's agreements and plan for the upcoming week.

The form below can be used for recording your weekly agreements.

Change List

Week of _____

1. I agree to _____

_____

2. I agree to _____

_____

3. I agree to _____

_____

4. I agree to _____

_____

Signature _____

Next Meeting _____
date   time

A Marriage Contract

As you work through the activities in this chapter, discussing issues that are common challenges and identifying ways to initiate changes in your relationship, you will begin to agree on basic principles that can govern your life together. It is a good idea to put these guidelines for your marriage into writing. Writing a contract helps you further clarify areas of agreement and disagreement and identify changes you desire that will require negotiation. In developing a marriage contract, all of the skills that you have been learning will be useful. A marriage contract is not a cold, legalistic document. Rather it is a set of guidelines that help a couple focus on their relationship in a positive way, a contract that demonstrates that the relationship is important enough to take the time and effort required to help it work.

Extending the Warranty on Your Marriage

No marriage can be made totally divorce-proof. There is sometimes a fine line between the things that make a marriage work and those that break it up. Equal marriage has no room for complacency. It requires both partners to take risks. The skills presented here will help you divorce-proof your marriage.

1. *Encourage each other often.* Make it a practice to encourage your partner daily. Nobody ever gets enough positive feedback. Encouraging each other seems simple. However, one of the most common complaints of partners is that they are not appreciated. In lasting relationships, partners make an effort to value and encourage one another. Encouragement can be incidental and spontaneous as well as planned. A partner who receives encouragement is more likely to give encouragement.

2. *Communicate openly and honestly with one another.* Be open and willing to share your thoughts and feelings, as well as to listen to your partner. Don't clam up or walk out on opportunities to grow and learn. Certain times are more appropriate than others for sharing. Sometimes it is wise to postpone a discussion,

as long as the purpose of the delay is not avoidance.

Certain times are more appropriate than others for sharing.

3. *Deal with conflict.* Life involves conflict. In healthy marriages, couples manage and respond to conflict in effective ways. Believe you can work out your problems together and take the time to do it. Use the conflict solution process.

4. *Develop the courage to be imperfect.* Be willing to apologize. The forgiveness process should not dwell on past grievances but should set the stage for greater harmony. "Where do we go from here?" is the question to ask after an apology. There is no need to keep the conflict going or to try to prove a point at this time. Accepting mistakes and problems as a normal part of married life can speed the transition to a satisfying marriage.

5. *Support each other fully.* Provide consistent and dependable support. Learn to suspend judgment and provide encouragement even when your partner's goals temporarily conflict with your own best interests.

6. *Develop regular times for fun each week.* Schedule time to be alone with each other. Fun should be a weekly, maybe even a daily activity.

7. *Choose to create a more satisfying relationship.* You are not a victim. You always have a choice.

8. *Develop shared dreams, goals, and interests.* Shared dreams and interests provide opportunities for conversation and mutual enjoyment. Couples with shared goals are less disturbed by minor or major crises.

9. *Be self-accepting.* The more you accept yourself, the more you will accept your partner. Mutual self-acceptance promotes both personal growth and growth of the relationship.

10. *Adopt realistic expectations.* Society fosters unrealistic, romantic expectations of marriage. Even in the best relationships some dreams and expectations are unfulfilled. Be honest and realistic when assessing your relationship.

In *Time for a Better Marriage* you have studied human behavior and learned procedures for improving your marital relationship. Even though you devote time and effort towards improvement, you will sometimes feel discouraged.

We tend to view growth and learning as progress along a diagonal line. Growth more closely resembles the incoming tide—we move forward, retreat, move further ahead, and then fall back. The loss of ground is discouraging if we don't realize that when we move forward we are a little ahead of where we were previously.

The priorities and expectations of marriage have changed considerably over the years. Many of our needs can be met outside of marriage. We can purchase services that eliminate certain responsibilities in order to take on other responsibilities. Marriage endures because two needs remain that cannot be met through casual relationships nor can they be purchased. These are the needs for love and commitment.

Marriage Maintenance Checklist

I am doing this more:

____ Understanding my goals and my partner's goals
____ Encouraging
____ Listening
____ Being empathic
____ Finding positive alternative meanings
____ Communicating honestly
____ Accepting responsibility for my self-esteem
____ Accepting responsibility for my feelings
____ Sharing my intentions
____ Having marriage meetings
____ Having encouragement meetings
____ Making choices
____ Resolving conflicts
____ Working to develop an equal relationship

I am doing this less:

____ Being unaware of goals
____ Discouraging
____ Ignoring
____ Not recognizing feelings
____ Being pessimistic or rigid
____ Not communicating honestly
____ Blaming
____ Making excuses, fault-finding
____ Not revealing my goals
____ Failing to plan and to talk together
____ Discouraging interaction
____ Feeling I have no choices
____ Battling for myself
____ Focusing on winning

References

1. Clifford J. Sager and Bernice Hunt, *Intimate Partners: Hidden Patterns in Love Relationships*, (NY: McGraw-Hill, 1979).

Questions

1. Describe an equal marriage. What can *you* do to help create an equal marriage?

2. Why is it important to identify strong and weak areas in your marriage?

3. How can a marriage contract strengthen your relationship?

4. What can you do to divorce-proof your relationship? Be specific.

5. List the changes that you and your partner have made since beginning this program. Be specific.

Even in the best relationships
some dreams and expectations are unfulfilled.

1. If you want to improve your marriage you must be willing to change.

2. In an equal marriage, partners have equal rights to develop as persons and equal responsibilities for taking care of themselves, each other, and their children.

3. Use the following skills to divorce-proof your marriage:
   a. Encourage each other often.
   b. Communicate frequently.
   c. Deal with conflict.
   d. Develop the courage to be imperfect.
   e. Support each other fully.
   f. Spend regular time together having fun.
   g. Be aware of choices you can make in your relationship.
   h. Develop shared dreams, goals, and interests.
   i. Be self-accepting.
   j. Have realistic expectations.

4. Recognize what is right with your marriage. Continue actions that currently please you and your partner.

5. Identify specific changes that you want to see in your marriage.

6. Decide what basic principles will govern your life together. Include these guidelines in a marriage contract.

7. Use the *Marriage Maintenance Checklist* to keep track of your progress in applying the skills presented in *Time for a Better Marriage*.

MY ◆ PLAN

Ways I can encourage _____

_____

Strengths I can use to improve the relationship _____

_____

Ways I can show I care or appreciate _____

_____

Ways I can improve my communication _____

_____

Effective ways I can resolve conflict _____

_____

I am ready and willing to change my behavior in the following way(s): _____

_____

MY PROGRESS IN APPLYING THESE SKILLS	I am doing this more	I need to do this more	I remain about the same
Listening to feelings			
Communicating honestly			
Encouraging			
Daily dialogue			
Communicating love			
Encouragement meetings			
Marriage meetings			
Resolving conflict effectively			
Demonstrating specific caring behavior			
Choosing a better marriage			
Spending time with my partner			

To Learn More About Training in Marriage Enrichment (TIME)

Time for a Better Marriage is the resource book for TRAINING IN MARRIAGE ENRICHMENT (*TIME*), a systematic, skill-development program conducted in a group setting. *TIME* helps couples better understand their marriage and at the same time helps them acquire the skills that make marriage effective, rewarding, and satisfying.

TRAINING IN MARRIAGE ENRICHMENT incorporates the sound principles and philosophy used so successfully in other programs authored by Dr. Dinkmeyer—STEP (Systematic Training for Effective Parenting), STEP/Teen, and STET (Systematic Training for Effective Teaching).

TIME can be used in many settings

- ten-session marriage enrichment program, with each session focusing on a specific skill

- intensive weekend workshop or retreat

- the beginning experience for an ongoing marriage support group

- church study groups, adult education programs, and university courses in family life, home economics, and counselor training

- workshops or individual sessions related to a specific *TIME* skill (encouragement or conflict resolution, for example)

- material for marriage counselors to use to supplement therapy

TIME Group Leadership

Who leads *TIME* groups?

- persons trained in the helping professions—psychologists, psychiatrists, social workers, counselors, priests, ministers, rabbis, educators, youth development workers, nurses, physicians

- lay persons able to facilitate discussion groups and willing to become thoroughly familiar with the principles and techniques presented in the *Leader's Guide* for *TIME*

- persons who have led STEP and STEP/Teen groups

TIME in Your Community

To receive information about *TIME* study groups in your area or how to become a *TIME* leader, write to the publisher:

TIME Coordinator
AGS
Publishers' Building
Circle Pines, MN 55014-1796

In Canada, write to:
Psycan Ltd.
101 Amber Street
Markham, Ontario L3R 3B2

In Australia, write to:
Australian Council for
Educational Research Ltd.
P.O. Box 210
Hawthorn, Victoria 3122

ENRICH II

David H. Olson's
marriage inventory

For more than five years marriage counselors have used the PREPARE/ENRICH inventories in both premarital and marital counseling with more than 30,000 couples. Now, ENRICH II is available for use with TIME marriage groups.

D o you and your partner see eye-to-eye on most issues affecting your marriage relationship? Often partners' perceptions of their marriage differ more than they realize. ENRICH II lets couples know how each partner views their relationship. This 125-item inventory pinpoints relationship strengths as well as work areas in the following categories: personality issues, communication, conflict resolution, financial management, sexual relationship, children and marriage, family and friends, equalitarian roles, religious orientation. The couple's relationship is described in terms of marital satisfaction, marital adaptability (how they deal with change), and marital cohesion (how they balance togetherness and separateness). Research has shown that without balance, both adaptability and cohesion can cause problems in a marriage relationship.

And the ENRICH II option for *TIME* groups helps couples apply the valuable skills learned in *Training In Marriage Enrichment* to the work

areas identified by the ENRICH II inventory. A special booklet details how the feedback from ENRICH II can be used in your marriage meetings to help you achieve a richer, more satisfying marriage.

ENRICH II is not a test. It cannot predict the success or failure of your marriage. Rather, it is a computer-scored inventory that provides feedback to the couple by means of a computer printout detailing areas of agreement and disagreement, areas of indecision, and special focus items that need to be addressed if a couple wants to achieve greater satisfaction in their marriage.

To learn more about *TIME* and ENRICH II, speak with your *TIME* group leader or contact the publisher:
American Guidance Service
Publishers' Building
Circle Pines, MN 55014-1796

Time to Relax and Imagine

Now by listening to *Time to Relax and Imagine* you can tap your inner resources to help you enrich your marriage. This personal audiocassette contains exercises in relaxation, self- encouragement, and relationship development as well as guided imagery exercises to enrich your marriage.

To receive your personal copy of *Time to Relax and Imagine,* fill in the order blank below:

- -

Please send _____ (no. copies) of *Time to Relax and Imagine* @ $7.00 per audiocassette to:

Total value of order $_____

_____
name

Service charge $3.00 if total value is less than $15.00 $_____

_____
address

Taxes if applicable $_____

_____
city, state, zip

(_____)_____
phone

GRAND TOTAL $_____

Send this form and your remittance to:
TIME Coordinator
AGS
Publishers' Building
Circle Pines, MN 55014-1796

OR,
phone toll free 1-800-328-2560
In Minnesota, call collect 1-612-786-4343

NOTES

NOTES

NOTES

NOTES

NOTES

NOTES

NOTES